Preaching
Jesus Christ
TODAY

Preaching Jesus Christ TODAY

Six Questions for Moving from Scripture to Sermon

ANNETTE BROWNLEE

Baker Academic
a division of Baker Publishing Group
Grand Rapids, Michigan

Published by Baker Academic
a division of Baker Publishing Group
PO Box 6287, Grand Rapids, MI 49516-6287
www.bakeracademic.com

Printed in the United States of America

Library of Congress Cataloging-in-Publication Data
Names: Brownlee, Annette, 1955– author.
Title: Preaching Jesus Christ today : six questions for moving from scripture to sermon / Annette Brownlee.
Description: Grand Rapids : Baker Publishing Group, 2018. | Includes bibliographical references and index.
Identifiers: LCCN 2017049009 | ISBN 9780801098826 (pbk.)
Subjects: LCSH: Preaching. | Bible—Homiletical use.
Classification: LCC BV4211.3 .B766 2018 | DDC 251—dc23
LC record available at https://lccn.loc.gov/2017049009

18 19 20 21 22 23 24   7 6 5 4 3 2 1

For he is our God,
and we are the people of his pasture,
and the sheep of his hand.
O that today you would listen to his voice!
Do not harden your hearts, as at Meribah,
as on the day at Massah in the wilderness,
when your ancestors tested me,
and put me to the proof,
though they had seen my work.
Psalm 95:7–9

For E, H, and I

Contents

Preface

Several years ago our daughter gave her father and me a small book for Christmas, *The Asian Grocery Store Demystified*. As the title suggests, the book takes the reader through the many unfamiliar vegetables and fruits sold in Asian markets and explains what they are and what to do with them in the kitchen. We love this book. We had recently moved to Toronto and bought a house near little Chinatown, just a block from its overflowing markets of strange fruits, vegetables, dried plants, and seafood. We cooked with the book, and over time we moved from sautéing bok choy and Japanese eggplant to cooking amaranth and fuzzy melon. We love it all.

Though the analogy is limited, it offers guidelines for a theologically shaped practice of preaching Jesus Christ. It points the way for preachers to have more confidence in their knowledge of what to do in the strange world of Scripture's fruits and nuts. To claim Scripture as God's word to us—to claim it as authoritative in the church and in our lives—is only a beginning for preachers. We preachers often need help in knowing what to do with these commitments in our sermons, especially in a world in which this claim carries little currency. The guidelines that follow take the form of six straightforward questions for listening to Scripture as one prepares sermons, week after week, and for moving from interpretation to sermon text in the midst of daily congregational life.

The inspiration for these guidelines comes out of the specific nature of the claim I am making: preaching Jesus Christ is a theological practice. Let me briefly say four things this claim implies, all of which I explore in the chapters to come.

First, preaching is theological. It is based on a variety of theological commitments, implicit or explicit, that shape how we read Scripture, preach from it, and move from Scripture to sermon in the context of worship and the church. As later chapters describe, these commitments have to do with what kind of text the preacher understands Scripture to be, the role of the church both in God's purposes for creation and in the interpretation of Scripture, questions of the correlation or connection between Scripture and our worlds today, between then and now, and the role of the preacher in the pulpit and in the congregation. The chief theological claim on which this practice rests is this: the location of preaching in and for the church needs to be the primary business of preachers and must shape how they go about sermon preparation. Why? The church is the God-given soil in which Scripture, preacher, and people are rooted, and the Spirit uses Scripture to testify to the church and to form it into the Spirit's witness to the nations. How might this theological claim shape how we as preachers read Scripture in sermon preparation, craft our sermons, understand our role, and use doctrine and personal stories? How does it shape our understanding of the role of sermons in discipleship and mission? These are questions this book addresses.

This project is part of the movement of theological retrieval that began with the postliberal theology of George Lindbeck and Hans Frei and has, more recently, moved into evangelical traditions.[1] This is not primarily a book of theology; it is about one approach to the practice of preaching based on theological commitments about Scripture and the church that have been part of this movement. It is anchored, in part, in a retrieval of David Yeago's understanding of the inspiration of Scripture, which is based not on plenary inspiration but on the Spirit's use of Scripture in the church for God's ongoing mission.[2]

1. See W. David Buschart and Ken D. Eilers, *Theology as Retrieval: Receiving the Past, Renewing the Church* (Downers Grove, IL: IVP Academic, 2015), for an excellent introduction to "retrieval" from an evangelical perspective.

2. George Lindbeck, *The Nature of Doctrine: Religion and Theology in a Postliberal Age* (Louisville: Westminster John Knox, 2009); George Lindbeck, *The Church in a Postliberal*

Second, preaching is a practice. It is one practice among many in the church, all of which are a response to God's gracious action through the Spirit. The nature of this response in preaching is that preachers need to *do* something with their interpretation of Scripture. Sermons involve a lot of movement—from Scripture to sermon, from the beginning of a sermon to its end, from the preacher's mouth to the people's ears to everyone's lives, from the gathered community out into the places people spend their weeks—all in the context of worship and a specific culture. It doesn't matter whether pastors preach from a written text, from notes, or just wing it or whether they preach in a Baptist church, an Anglican church, or a café. This movement is not primarily about sermon form, literary style, or holding the listener's (and the preacher's) interest. It is about the power of God on the cross to bring into existence that which is not. In the synagogue in Thessalonica, Paul preaches about this power, the Messiah who suffers and rises from the dead; and what is the reaction of some who hear? They say, "These people . . . have been turning the world upside down" and send a mob in search of Paul and Silas (Acts 17:1–7; here v. 6).

Preachers need help knowing what to do with their theological commitments in their interpretation of Scripture and how to serve it up in a sermon. In my claim that preaching is a theological practice, I aim to expand the movement of theological retrieval to include not only the interpretation of Scripture but also the interpretation of Scripture for the practice of preaching.

Third, preaching is a theologically shaped practice of proclaiming Jesus Christ. This statement shows my theological hand. All Scripture reveals the risen and ascended Jesus Christ. In Scripture, through the Spirit, Christ addresses us individually and as a people; and, again through the Spirit, we are able to respond. Preachers do not have to figure out on their own how to make Scripture meaningful or relevant. Jesus Christ is implicitly relevant and is the meaning and telos of our lives and of all creation. However, preachers do need help in knowing how to pay attention to Scripture; how to see Jesus Christ, the son of

---

Age, ed. James J. Buckley (Grand Rapids: Eerdmans, 2003); David S. Yeago, "The Bible: The Spirit, the Church and the Scriptures; Biblical Inspiration and Interpretation Revisited," in *Knowing the Triune God: The Work of the Spirit in the Practices of the Church*, 49–93, ed. James J. Buckley and David S. Yeago (Grand Rapids: Eerdmans, 2001).

the God of Israel, revealed there; and then how to listen with and on behalf of their congregations as God addresses them through it. We preachers need help knowing what it looks like to be the people God makes us through Christ's address to us in our particular contexts.

Finally, preaching and sermon preparation are practices of pastors. To say this is not to imply for a moment that this happens in isolation. Preachers prepare sermons from within and for their communities; preachers are part of their interpretative communities. With their congregations, pastors are called to stand under God's Word and let it address them. We are called to close the gap between pastors, in their authoritative role, and people. What distinguishes the preacher from her congregation is her role; and for most of us, the weekly round of sermon preparation is a key practice in our God-given vocation of binding ourselves to God's people and to God's Word for the sake of God's world. Here I invite preachers to see sermon preparation as a key spiritual practice in their ongoing growth in Christ through this vocational binding. To do so I turn to Augustine. In *On Christian Teaching* he writes of the relationship between sticking with the hard parts of Scripture and loving feeble, difficult people. The same skill is needed for both. The discipline needed to stick with both the concrete words of Scripture (what is often called the textually mediated world of Scripture) and the fleshly limitations of the human condition is an ability to see the redemption of both in Christ's incarnation.[3] This is our call as pastors: to see Jesus Christ as we are bound to God's Word and to God's people for the sake of God's redemption for the world.

Why does any of this matter? The hallmark of this postmodern age, where differences between people—the other—are regularly perceived in terms of struggles for power and contested realities, is that it lends itself to preaching abstract principles and timeless propositions or retreating to personal stories, all of which are easier to swallow. Love, justice, and justification seem broad enough ideas—we hope—with room for everyone across social, educational, racial, sexual, and geographic divisions. Preaching universal principles or resorting to personal stories, however, is not preaching Jesus Christ, incarnate, risen,

3. Augustine, *On Christian Teaching (On Christian Doctrine)*, trans. R. P. H. Green (Oxford: Oxford University Press, 1999), 27–28.

ascended, and coming again. Paul asks, "*Who* will rescue me from this body of death?" (Rom. 7:24). Not *what*. The good news of the gospel is that Christ's incarnation into the problematic particularity of the human condition is this fallen world's redemption. In his incarnation Christ embraces the differences and inequalities that are part of being human, a creature in a particular time and place. In this embrace he offers us not a way to negate the chasms between ourselves and others, or a way to define them in terms of a struggle for dominance, but a way to love across the gaps. In what follows I endeavor to show that an attentive reading of Scripture, hard parts and all, focusing on the identity that Jesus Christ offers, gives us a way to preach—and most importantly to love—in a postmodern world.

Is this not our hope, that Jesus Christ is the way, the truth, and the life *across* all our contested realities? That he speaks in all times, cultures, and places? The burden of making Jesus relevant in our time and context is too heavy for even the most gifted preacher. But before preachers open their mouths or Bibles, God has created the condition for us to be able to preach Jesus Christ. What is that? God has created us able to hear his Word. All of us, across centuries, continents, and cultures. All of us together. Only God can create hearers of his Word, Luther claims; and God has done just that through the Holy Spirit.[4] Thus preaching truly is first and last a response to the gracious action of the Spirit, which makes us able to hear God's Word. As Augustine writes, before we are preachers we are hearers of the Word.[5] Before we can be preachers we must listen to God's Word along with our people. This is who God has made us. The psalmist writes, "Hear this, all you peoples; / give ear, all inhabitants of the world, / both low and high, rich and poor together" (Ps. 49:1–2).

Such is our privilege: to learn to listen to the Word with those God has entrusted to us in our congregations. Our vocation as preachers is found in this: to stand under the Word with our people, in the context of the church, and to let it address and shape us.

---

4. All citations from the works of Martin Luther are taken from Martin Luther, *Luther's Works* (American edition), ed. Jaroslav Pelikan and Helmut T. Lehmann, 55 vols. (St. Louis: Concordia, 1955–86); here, *Sermons on the Gospel of St. John Chapters 1–4*, 22:8.

5. Paul Kolbet, *Augustine and the Cure of Souls: Revising a Classical Ideal* (Notre Dame, IN: University of Notre Dame Press, 2010), 208.

The Organization of the Book

The book is organized around the Six Questions of the Sermon. The introduction lays out what is at stake if we lose the practice of carefully attending to Scripture for proclamation, and it roots the Six Questions and the role of the preacher in the common life of the church. The heart of the book moves through the Six Questions in order. With each specific question I discuss the theological and hermeneutical issues it brings to the foreground, the role of the preacher in this stage of sermon preparation, and tools for using the questions in sermon preparation. Each question is set in its postmodern context. The final section of the book offers sample sermons using the Six Questions.

The Six Questions of a Theologically Shaped Practice of Preaching Jesus Christ

1. What do I see? The preacher as witness.

   ▶ Main action: Attentively read the appointed Scriptures.

2. Whom do I see? The preacher as witness to Christ.

   ▶ Main action: Describe the identity of Jesus Christ revealed in the text.

3. What is Christ's word to me? The preacher as confessor.

   ▶ Main action: Hear God's address to you and receive God's mercy and judgment.

4. What is Christ's word to us? The preacher as theologian.

   ▶ Main action: Hear God's address to the church and one's own congregation in its particular context.

5. What is Christ's word about us? The preacher as theologian of a broken body.

   ▶ Main action: Describe the identity of the church and the disciple given in Christ's word and address to us.

6. What does it look like? The preacher as witness to Christ in a disobedient world.

   ▶ Main action: Facilitate recognition of how the identity of Christ is inhabited in a broken and disobedient world.

The Six Questions move from attentiveness to the scriptural text (What do I see?); to the text's center and completion, Jesus Christ (Whom do I see?); to Christ's address to us personally (What is Christ's word to me?); to Christ's address to us as the church (What is Christ's word to us?); to the identity Christ offers the church and disciples (What is Christ's word about us?); to how we inhabit our identity in Christ for and in a disobedient world (What does it look like?).

Acknowledgments

There are many people whose fingerprints are on these pages. I am grateful to all of them. Philip Turner read an early version. Ellen Davis and Will Willimon provided early support. Dave Nelson at Baker Academic provided excellent advice about the organization of the book. Melisa Blok, my editor at Baker, made this a better book. Rachel Lott proofed the manuscript and tracked down errant citations. My colleagues at Wycliffe College and the Toronto School of Theology provided steady encouragement, and clergy friends in Kingston were willing to practice using these questions for a summer of sermons. Colleagues at the Academy of Homiletics provided constructive feedback to portions of chapters. But primarily I am in the debt of the congregations with whom, over the years, I have broken bread and tried to hear and respond to God's Word. To the people of St. Paul's in East Cleveland, Ohio; St. Luke's in Cleveland, Ohio; Emmanuel in Stamford, Connecticut; Ascension in Pueblo, Colorado; St. Paul's L'Amoreaux in Scarborough, Toronto; and Founder's Chapel in Wycliffe College, Toronto. Many thanks to those who gave me permission to use their stories. Finally I am thankful for my husband, who has been with me through it all.

Introduction

Listening to Scripture for Preaching:
A Discipline in Need of Remediation

I recently heard a sermon on Zephaniah 1:7, 12–18. This text about the day of the Lord, in which neither gold nor silver will save the complacent from the Lord's wrath—that is, from having their blood "poured out like dust, and their flesh like dung"—is part of the Revised Common Lectionary assigned at the end of November in Year A. The preacher is commended for not avoiding this tough Old Testament text; though the Gospel assigned for the same Sunday, Matthew 25:14–30, is no more congenial. In the Gospel a certain master throws one of the servants he entrusted with his property into the outer darkness, amid weeping and gnashing of teeth. The preacher could have preached on the psalm or the reading from 1 Thessalonians. Rather, he bravely tackled this difficult text. Except he really didn't. Instead he preached around its edges. He spoke of the difficulty of the text. He pointed to Zephaniah 1:1, which speaks of the need for silence before the Lord. He promised his listeners that this text would be easier to deal with when it came up in the lectionary in Advent, with the chapter's beginning verses. He located this reading contextually in the rest of Zephaniah. But each time the preacher turned toward the content of the passage assigned for this particular Sunday, he quickly exited its dark contours by telling

1

an amusing story or an anecdote, which turned our attention away from its particular challenges.

A Quick Exit from Scripture's Room

What I heard on that particular Sunday in November is not uncommon. Because preachers aren't necessarily sure how to listen to Scripture—let alone how to serve it up in a sermon that is life giving to those who then listen to it—we quickly skip over its difficulties. We leave its foreign world for the more familiar and accessible world of story and personal experience. A fellow preacher told me, "I'm a storyteller by nature and use lots of stories in my preaching, and yet I have an uneasy feeling about the connection between my stories and the Scripture."

Stories and personal experience are not our only way of evading Scripture's strangeness. I work at Wycliffe College at the University of Toronto, an evangelical-Anglican seminary composed of students from Anglican/Episcopal and other Protestant traditions. This denominational soup, while maintaining its Anglican heritage and form of worship, is united by a commitment to the enduring Word of God and the inheritance of the Reformed tradition. All would confess, in some way or another, that Scripture is God's enduring, authoritative, and living word.

A commitment to the authority of Scripture, however, is no guarantee that preachers will know what to do with it in a sermon. These evangelical students are no surer of how to read Scripture than those who may not identify as evangelical. What to do with its historical particularity, the place of historical criticism in their interpretation, their own faith—and what to do with all of this in a sermon? They frequently exit the text of Scripture and turn to doctrine, pietism, moral exhortation, and personal experience in order to proclaim it. So, for example, they might rest their shaky sermons on theological truisms such as grace, justification, and repentance, which are important terms but ones many parishioners drop in the recycling boxes as they leave church. Often, without meaning to do so, preachers of all kinds exit Scripture's room through storytelling, personal experience, doctrine, and piety; in doing so, they walk away from Scripture's rich fruits.

Whom Do We Blame?

I don't think we can lay this tendency to exit Scripture's room on the backs of individual clergy and their inability to manage their time or on those who teach preaching or even on the ease of downloading sermons. There has been an erosion of confidence in the power of the gospel. The erosion is partly due to decreasing confidence in Christian language and practices, but also to the lack of practice in carefully reading and listening to Scripture. In the introduction to *The Art of Reading Scripture*, the authors describe reading Scripture as a form of art, a creative discipline that requires engagement and imagination. They go on to acknowledge that it is difficult to do well and that "the disciplines of attentiveness to the word do not come easily to us."[1] It is a discipline in need of remediation.

Scripture's Authority and Particularity

Two central characteristics of Scripture are problematic for many at this time: its authority and its historical particularity. Is it surprising that we don't know what to do with it? Both the authority of Scripture and the church's basic practices (which spring from it) are called first-order language and practices—and they are contested.[2] Many denominations have divided or are in division over differing understandings of baptism, Holy Communion, marriage, ordination, and the interpretation of Scripture.[3] "Religions," George Lindbeck writes, "have become

1. Ellen F. Davis and Richard B. Hays, *The Art of Reading Scripture* (Grand Rapids: Eerdmans, 2003), xv. They then go on to lay out nine theses for how to read Scripture with imagination, engagement, and attentiveness (1–5). The essays included in the volume flesh these out for the life of the church and for preaching.

2. Beginning with the Reformation, disagreements between Catholics and Protestants over the relationship between church and Scripture led to an erosion of confidence in both. The clarity of Scripture and the teaching role of the church became places of competing claims and discord. For a fuller historical investigation of this erosion, see Ephraim Radner, "The Absence of the Comforter: Scripture and the Divided Church," in *Theological Exegesis: Essays in Honor of Brevard S. Childs*, ed. Christopher Seitz and Kathryn Greene-McCreight (Grand Rapids: Eerdmans, 1999), 355–94.

3. Here I mention marks of the church. Others include prayer, worship, discipleship, evangelism, and mission. Martin Luther describes seven basic marks of the church in *Luther's Works*, 41:148–68. For a more comprehensive understanding of practices in the church, see Miroslav Volf and Dorothy C. Bass, eds., *Practicing Theology: Beliefs and*

foreign texts that are much easier to translate into current popular categories than to read in terms of their intrinsic sense."[4] They have also become battlegrounds. Augustine's claim that what is written in the Scriptures is better and truer—even if its meaning is hidden—than anything we could think of by ourselves seems preposterous to some and scandalous to others.[5]

In *Preaching and the Other*, Ronald Allen writes, "To be postmodern is to respect difference and otherness, to appreciate pluralism and particularity, and to recognize the social conditioning and relativity of all awareness."[6] However, to acknowledge and respect the particularity of the other, as Allen describes, does not necessarily mean we know what to do with it in our congregations, the world, or our sermons. What do I do with the texts about circumcision? In Scripture it is a practice only for men, and in contemporary practice, female circumcision is a form of mutilation and is against the law in most countries where it occurs (though laws are poorly enforced). What do I do with Jesus's conversation with the woman caught in adultery? Where is the man who was part of her act?

Particularity is part of the sunk cost of being a creature. I cannot be born and shaped everywhere or anywhere. Neither can you. By the fact of being creatures we are unequal in most of the ways we measure the human race: economic, social, educational, ecological, and so on. This raises difficult questions for the practice of preaching. Can I speak for anyone but myself in a sermon? Do I have a right to speak for or about others? I assist at a church in Scarborough, a part of Toronto considered one of the most ethnically diverse neighborhoods in the world. Can I preach the same sermon to all my parishioners, many of whom are immigrants from places as varied as mainland China, Sri Lanka, Ghana, and the Bahamas? If so, how? Unsure of what to do with their particularity, as well as my own and that of Scripture—and wanting to respect differences—I am often tempted to recast texts and situations

---

Practices in Christian Life (Grand Rapids: Eerdmans, 2001), and Dorothy C. Bass, *Practicing Our Faith: A Way of Life for a Searching People* (San Francisco: Jossey-Bass, 1997). The latter explores twelve Christian practices, from honoring the body to household economics.

4. Lindbeck, *Nature of Doctrine*, 110.

5. Augustine, *On Christian Teaching* 2.7.9.

6. Ronald J. Allen, *Preaching and the Other: Studies of Postmodern Insights* (St. Louis: Chalice, 2009), 15.

that seem primarily contextual into abstract or universalized terms like love, tolerance, or hope. Otherwise they might become contested and reduced to struggles for power. It is easy to see the appeal of leaving Scripture's stubborn detail and asking instead, "What do these words mean to me?" or "What do they express about me?" Or of jumping from Scripture into a sermon on justice or justification by faith. Or of telling a story.

But there is something of a vicious circle in this uncertainty over what to do with Scripture's stubborn particularity. The lack of practice in carefully reading and listening to Scripture leads to an erosion of confidence in the church and Scripture as primary vessels of the Spirit's saving work in the world—a result that only decreases our attention to it. L. Gregory Jones makes just this point. He notes that the rise in arguments about various methods of reading and interpreting Scripture is, in part, due to the declining practice of actually reading it.[7] He states, "Even evangelicals, who have a very high view of the Bible's authority, often have a rather low competence in reading and embodying Scripture."[8]

In light of the difficulties with the particularity of Scripture and contested church practices, the turn to doctrine, piety, or the more accessible and less contested world of stories and personal experience in the search for meaning is appealing. This is especially true when the rhythm of parish ministry crowds out time for much else. But in doing so, we have exited Scripture's room without realizing it. We look around it quickly then walk to the nearest exit to find its meaning.

A Quick Exit from Scripture: An Example

I offer the following by way of example: Say I am preaching on Christ's temptations in the wilderness from either Luke or Matthew. I focus on how Christ's temptations show us that God is always with us when we are tempted. In doing so, I have exited the particularities of *Christ's* temptations—as specific to him—and have stepped into the world of human temptation. I have interpreted Christ's battles with the

---

7. L. Gregory Jones, "Embodying Scripture in the Community of Faith," in Davis and Hays, *Art of Reading Scripture*, 143–47.

8. Jones, "Embodying Scripture," 145.

devil in the wilderness in terms of a shared experience of temptation between Christ, me, and my parishioners.

Or, perhaps I take the text in a different direction. I preach that Christ's temptations in the wilderness show us how God responds to our obedience. I go on to apply this teaching on obedience to everyday situations my congregation confronts in the wildernesses of their own lives. I interpret the particularities of Christ's battle in terms of a generalized teaching about obedience.

Notice what has happened in these examples. I have preached sermons that are worth hearing, since it is true that God is with us in our temptations and that disciples are called to obedience. I have tried to offer my congregation comfort, hope, and direction. But I could have preached either sermon without this specific text. The details of Christ's temptations, the uncomfortable statement that the Spirit drove Jesus out into the wilderness, the angels ministering to Jesus, and the devil's promise to come again at an opportune time are skipped over. What the details of this text say about who Jesus is has been left for another time. In both cases, because of my desire to make the Scripture speak to my congregation, I have looked outside of it for its meaning: in a shared experience, in a church teaching. I have exited Scripture's room and its rich and stubborn detail.

The Six Questions of the Sermon and a Turn to the Church

Facing an erosion of confidence in Scripture and in practices of the church, we desire to preach sermons that speak to our congregations. But we do not have to turn away from Scripture's particularity in order to make it meaningful. Along with the first disciples, we say to Jesus, "To whom can we go? You have the words of eternal life" (John 6:68). These words of eternal life, however, God gives to us in the often difficult and obscure words of Scripture. As R. R. Reno has eloquently stated, an erosion of confidence in the gospel calls us not to look away from Scripture and the practices of the church, but to look again— attentively, expectantly, and obediently.

> We should not try to ignore or correct or deny the spiritual dryness of the *concreta Christiana*. The difficulties are quite real. . . . But precisely

as such, the difficulties and impediments are constitutive of the very saving power of Jesus Christ. The impotence we perceive is part of the potency of new life that is promised, for it forces us to submit ourselves to a lifetime of obedient searching in the very *concreta Christiana* we might so quickly abandon as inauspicious and lifeless. The weakness forces us to look again rather than to look elsewhere.[9]

The Six Questions of the Sermon provide the structure for this book and act as guidelines to help the preacher do just this: to look attentively at Scripture and understand how to interpret and preach what she sees. To do so, the Six Questions distill a theologically shaped practice of preaching Jesus Christ into its simplest form and clarify the preacher's role in each step. In other words, they are designed to be simple enough to be remembered and easy enough to be used. They spring from a commitment to Scripture as God's revealed word and address to the church (Rev. 3:22), a church that is given a specific identity, vocation, and mission by the one who addresses it and whose word creates it. The Six Questions are also shaped by the claim that the church—in which are located both Scripture and the people God forms through it—needs to be more than an afterthought to how we read, hear, interpret, and preach Scripture.

The questions, in their simplest form, are as follows:

What do I see? The preacher as witness.

Whom do I see? The preacher as witness to Christ.

What is Christ's word to me? The preacher as confessor.

What is Christ's word to us? The preacher as theologian.

What is Christ word about us? The preacher as theologian of a broken body.

What does it look like? The preacher as witness to Christ in a disobedient world.

The Six Questions of the Sermon return the reading and interpretation of Scripture for preaching to the church. Why the church? The

---

9. Russell Reno, *In the Ruins of the Church: Sustaining Faith in an Age of Diminished Christianity* (Grand Rapids: Brazos, 2002), 144.

church is the soil in which Scripture, preacher, and congregation are rooted. In other words, the church is the natural habitat for interpreting Scripture for proclamation. It is the place where, over the centuries, Scripture is heard, proclaimed, and lived. Thus to develop a theologically shaped practice of preaching I offer guidelines for hearing Scripture as God's address to us, personally and corporately, and for receiving the identity God offers us in Jesus Christ in the church. We enact this identity, in response to Christ's address to us, in and for the broken and disobedient world.

The Ecosystem of the Church

Several years ago on a Sunday afternoon, amid one of my parish's annual fundraisers for mission work, I received a call to come immediately to the hospital. There had been an accident at a parishioner's home and the infant of a parishioner was not breathing. The doctors and nurses tried to revive the child but were unable to do so. The parents wanted me to baptize their baby before the nurses called the time of death. It is one of the hardest things we do as clergy. I did so amid the overflowing love in that room, as the baby's mother and father held it, the nurses competently kept an eye on the situation, and we all wept. A few days later her parents carried an infant-sized coffin into a full church for the funeral, and afterward we all drove to the family gravesite outside of town for the committal. It was a long, heart-wrenching week. I did not expect the family to be in church that Sunday. But there they were: father, mother, a sibling. I was in the pulpit and they were in the congregation—trying to listen. What could they possibly hear?

As a parish pastor I have learned that there is a vital relationship between what happens in the pulpit and what happens in the rest of parish life. This organic relationship involves the proclamation of the Word in sermon, sacrament, and practices of the church. It involves the individual listeners in their many contexts and backgrounds, the communities beyond the church of which parishioners are a part, and the building up of a corporate sense of identity in the church as a visible witness in the world to the new life given in Jesus Christ (Eph. 1–3). In the body of Christ I have learned that one cannot separate the hospital room, the pulpit, the local jail, the neighborhood, and the mission trip or field any more than the eye can say to the hand, "I have no need of you." Pastors and congregants know that sermons are only one part of this ecosystem, though connected to all the others.[10] The complex ecosystem of the church—not personal experience, abstract principles, piety, or doctrine—is the soil in which both Scripture and God's people are rooted.

This claim rests on the promise that the Spirit uses Scripture to build the church. We sing of this hope in the hymn "The Church's One Foundation": "She is his new creation by water and the Word." The homiletician Richard Eslinger has described the Spirit's use of Scripture to build the church as a "double movement."[11] Eslinger reiterates Stanley Hauerwas's claim that the biblical story "is not self-referential but rather creates a people capable of being a continuation of the narrative by witnessing to the world that all creation is ordered for God's good end. The church is the necessary context for the testing of that narrative."[12] Thus the Spirit uses Scripture to build the church by creating a people able to hear and respond to it. The focus of Scripture is not on God's being in and of itself—for that is not the story found in the canon—but on "how life is to be lived and reality construed in the light of God's character as an agent as this is depicted in the stories of Israel and of Jesus."[13]

The church the Spirit builds is one capable of hearing and responding to Scripture in its common life and in the lives of disciples in the world. Not perfectly, not without great failures, but nonetheless able to hear and respond. Thus the church is not only the soil in which Scripture and people are rooted; it is not only a web or ecosystem of relationships and practices. Because the Spirit uses Scripture to create a people capable of hearing it, *God has made the church the primary form of the interpretation of Scripture.* A commitment to the life, activity, and

10. David Lose notes this and comments that it takes some of the burden off what a sermon must accomplish. See *Confessing Jesus Christ: Preaching in a Postmodern World* (Grand Rapids: Eerdmans, 2003).

11. Richard Eslinger, *Narrative and Imagination: Preaching the Worlds That Shape Us* (Minneapolis: Fortress, 1995), 30.

12. Eslinger, *Narrative and Imagination,* 26, quoting Stanley Hauerwas. See Hauerwas, "The Church as God's New Language," in *Scriptural Authority and Narrative Interpretation,* ed. Garrett Green (Philadelphia: Fortress, 1987), 183.

13. Lindbeck, *Nature of Doctrine,* 121.

organization of the Christian community is the fundamental form of
the interpretation of Scripture.[14] In Paul's Letter to the Ephesians, he
writes of the church's key role in the plan of God, who created all things.
"Through the church the wisdom of God in its rich variety might now
be made known to the rulers and authorities in the heavenly places"
(3:10). In other words, the witness of the Spirit in the world is mediated not only through the words of Scripture but also through the life
of a people formed by the Word, Jesus Christ.

We do not have to exit Scripture, with its difficulties and particularities,
into the world of personal experience, abstract principles, doctrine, or piety
in order to interpret it for preaching. The actions, practices, identity, and
mission of the church, in its various expressions, *are* the meaning and
interpretation of Scripture, both in its common life and as believers go
about their lives as disciples in their own time and place.

The Eclipse of the Church in the West

Perhaps it seems like poor timing to develop an approach to preaching
based on the claim that the church is the primary form of the interpretation of Scripture, as the rapid decline of the church and its many divisions
in the West have dimmed its witness to Jesus Christ. But it is here, in the
face of the church's limitations and failures, that we should follow Reno's
advice. Rather than look away from or question the church's central place
in the plan of salvation as described in Ephesians (what was God thinking?), we should look again, attentively, obediently, and expectantly. To
do so thrusts us back, as Reno says, onto the narrow way of Jesus Christ.

That is where we need to be. The narrow way of Christ offers us
a way forward in the postmodern world of contested otherness. The
central identity of Jesus Christ is as one who has embraced particularity. Christ comes as a particular person in a particular time and
place. His incarnation compels us to resist capitulating to a conceptual
understanding of the Other or to reducing otherness to a struggle for
dominance. In the church our primary identity is found *within* Christ's
embrace and redemption of creaturely differences and inequalities.[15]

14. Nicholas Lash, *Theology on the Way to Emmaus* (London: SCM, 1986), 42.
15. Ephraim Radner, *Leviticus*, Brazos Theological Commentary on the Bible (Grand
Rapids: Brazos, 2008), 120–34.

The Cost of Turning Away from Scripture

The dangers of abandoning Scripture are far worse than the difficulties of knowing how to read it. The cost of turning away from it is simply too high in terms of the vocation God has given the church. In *Captive to the Word of God*, Miroslav Volf writes of the current resurgence of a theological reading of Scripture by both biblical scholars and systematic theologians, which he calls "the most significant theological development in the last two decades."[16] He places the importance of this resurgence in light of the eclipse of the theologian's role in shaping public life. "To the extent that theology is able to shape broader society at all, it will be able to do so *largely to the degree that it is able to shape the life of the Christian communities.*"[17] The vocation God gives to the church as a light to the world is not eclipsed despite the shrinking public role of the church in much of the West. Given this shrinkage, we have a great urgency to form persons who are shaped by the life of Jesus Christ through the common life of the church. Individual church communities and persons formed by them are the church's great way of participating in societies. Philip Turner insightfully declares that "the exemplary power of lives well lived" is perhaps a key way the church models the truth of the life and death of Jesus Christ today.[18]

Martin Luther King Jr. preached at a time when the church still had an influence on the larger society. But he also knew, as Richard Lischer describes in *The Preacher King*, that the congregation is at the center of Christianity.

> Ebenezer [Baptist Church] had taught King that the basic unit of Christianity in the world is the congregation.... Perhaps he understood that Christianity was never meant to work in the lecture hall or at the level of abstract principles but, rather, among a community that is joined by race, family, neighborhood, and economics, but whose truest identity transcends all of these.... The power of Jesus is in the church. The

16. Miroslav Volf, *Captive to the Word of God: Engaging the Scriptures for Contemporary Theological Reflection* (Grand Rapids: Eerdmans, 2010), 14.

17. Volf, *Captive to the Word of God*, 10 (emphasis original).

18. Philip Turner makes this point in *Christian Ethics and the Church: Ecclesial Foundations for Moral Thought and Practice* (Grand Rapids: Baker Academic, 2015). See the section "The Exemplary Power of Lives Well Lived: Truth and Reconciliation," 205–11.

congregation is the laboratory for the love commanded by God and the instrument of his justice. The black preacher knows that if it isn't happening there, it isn't happening.[19]

What we do in our congregations matters, even if it seems small, tedious, and fruitless at times. Our sermons matter. Our sermon preparation matters. So do our evangelism, ethics, outreach, formation, witness, and mission. Our people matter enormously. And communicating the gospel to them matters now even more than before.

The Role of the Preacher: Witness, Confessor, and Theologian

For each of the Six Questions of the Sermon, I describe the role the preacher assumes in that step of sermon preparation. I do so for two reasons. The first is to help the preacher use the Six Questions by offering two ways to understand and enter into each of them. Each question is meant to clarify the preacher's role, and the description of the role is meant to clarify the intent of the question. For example, in question 1 (What do I see? The preacher as witness), the preacher might ask herself, "What am I doing when I describe what I see in the text?" The role assigned to the preacher in question 1 helps her to answer her own question. I am being a witness. Or, with question 4 (What is Christ's word to me? The preacher as confessor), the preacher might ask herself, "What does it mean to be a confessor?" It means that I speak of my own faith and of my own response to standing under the Word and trying to hear Christ address me in it.

Second, the role of the preacher is shaped by the double movement of the Spirit: the Spirit uses Scripture to create a people able to hear and respond to it. The preacher is part of this interpretive community that the Spirit creates and has a particular role in it. The preacher is a witness. She attentively reads Scripture and sits with it until she can witness to the God who acts in and through it. The preacher is a confessor. As the Spirit makes both preacher and congregation able to hear and respond to Scripture, the preacher must allow herself to be addressed

---

19. Richard Lischer, *The Preacher King: Martin Luther King, Jr. and the Word That Moved America* (New York: Oxford University Press, 1997), 79.

by the one about whom she has witnessed. The preacher cannot be a witness to God and then stand outside the need to respond to the one she testified to. This one—the living God who raises the dead—calls forth from us a response, and the Spirit makes that response possible. Thus, the preacher must be a confessor as well as a witness. Finally, the preacher is a theologian. The Spirit uses Scripture to build the church, and the preacher speaks of the shared identity we are given for the sake of the world in Jesus Christ. Her witness and confession is not for herself alone. It is for her congregation and for building up the church's witness.

The Preacher's Ongoing Growth in Christ

A theologically shaped practice of preaching, rooted in the church, offers tired clergy a way to understand their sermon preparation as a central practice in their ongoing growth in Christ. Our vocation as pastors is to bind ourselves to God's Word and to God's people in the weekly rhythm of parish life. The vocation of the preacher is an odd one in an electronic age. Where else, except in houses of worship, do people gather together to listen to a person or persons speak, week after week? Not to movies, TED talks, or YouTube videos, but to a person? In *Preacher and Cross*, André Resner Jr. reminds us that speech is always tied to the one speaking; and for the Christian preacher, sermons are tied not to some general ethic of character but to his ethos or character as rooted in the cross of Jesus Christ.[20] In visual media—movies, videos, and images—the cord has been cut between the character of the messenger (actors, speakers, editors) and the message. This is not so in the act of preaching. As we preach, our character preaches as well, and more importantly, so does our stature in Jesus Christ. This is more important than eloquent words or finely crafted sermons.

The ease of downloading sermons or leaving our preparation to Saturday night might seem a necessary pastoral reality, but the discipline of attentively reading Scripture for sermon preparation is a key practice for clergy as they seek to grow in Christ. We cheat ourselves when our weeks crowd out this discipline. We also cheat those to whom

20. André Resner Jr., *Preacher and Cross: Person and Message in Theology and Rhetoric* (Grand Rapids: Eerdmans, 1999), 105–28.

we are bound in love. In *On Christian Teaching*, Augustine writes of the discipline we must develop in order to stay with the difficult parts of Scripture. He claims that the skills we need to read Scripture properly are also the very ones needed to act morally. To stick with both the strange world of Scripture and the limitations of the human condition is the same: we need to be able to see that both lead beyond themselves to Christ, who in his flesh has embraced and redeemed our limitations.[21] Can this not also help us to abide in the constraints and brokenness of our ministries and those of our congregations? Our people—like the all-too-human words of Scripture, which we stumble over and often prefer to ignore—lead beyond themselves to Jesus Christ. Developing the patience, trust, and discipline to become fluent in God's transforming Word, given in this life in the humble, broken speech of Scripture, helps us to develop the perceptive powers to look for and recognize Christ in creaturely finitude and flaws, including our own. It leads to a life where, rather than trying to transcend these limitations, we joyfully bind ourselves in love to God's Word, people, and world in obedient expectation. The attentive reading of Scripture for sermon preparation will be a primary spiritual discipline throughout our ministries. Our hope is that, over time, the Spirit will form us into people and pastors able to do just this.

Augustine as a Model for Preaching in a Postmodern World

Does Augustine, who prepared sermons in the fourth and fifth centuries, have anything helpful to say to those who preach in a culturally diverse church—in a pluralistic, postmodern, secular world—where many do not know the basic story of Scripture? He does, for his world was not unlike ours.

Immediately after his ordination as a priest, Augustine wrote a letter to his bishop, Valerius, asking for some time to study the Scriptures. Valerius had asked Augustine to preach regularly, even though at that time preaching was primarily restricted to bishops. Augustine felt he needed to study the Scriptures with an ear for how they speak to the whole church and not just to one man in the privacy of his

---

21. Augustine, *On Christian Teaching* 3.10.14. See also Kolbet, *Augustine and the Cure of Souls*, 150.

garden.[22] How could he preach to all his flock, the classically trained, the uneducated, and the pagans? How could he preach as their pastor? This is what he needed time to figure out. His dilemma is our dilemma. How do we preach to those who are suspicious of Scripture or who do not know its basic story? How do we preach to a wide range of needs, situations, and starting places? Across economic, educational, and ethnic lines? That Augustine was able to do so without excising Scripture of its content offers us a model and a challenge.

Augustine wrote what is considered the first Christian manual on preaching, *De doctrina christiana* or *On Christian Teaching*. He began writing it at the beginning of his episcopacy in the 390s but did not complete a portion of book 3 and all of book 4 until the end of his life in the late 420s. It is worth our attention to look at how this manual teaches preaching. Unlike many books on preaching, which begin with a definition of preaching or descriptions of the vocation of the preacher—as shepherd, pastor, herald, witness—Augustine begins in another place. He begins with this question: How do we learn Scripture? Three of the four books of *On Christian Teaching* are devoted to addressing this question. Only in the fourth book does he turn to the kinds of questions we usually associate with preaching: questions of form, rhetoric, persuasion, eloquence, and so on.

In the organization of *On Christian Teaching* Augustine presents the principle I consider essential to all Christian preaching: how we learn to read Scripture is absolutely fundamental, as is learning to read it for the vocation of preaching in the church. The preface to *On Christian Teaching* defends the legitimacy of teaching rules for interpreting Scripture. In it Augustine clearly states the connection between God's revealed Word and the divine means of passing it on, which defines the vocation of the preacher and pastor—to bind herself to God's Word and God's people.

> The human condition would be wretched indeed if God appeared unwilling to minister his word to human beings through human agency. . . . Moreover, there would be no way for love, which ties people together in the bonds of unity, to make souls overflow and as

22. Peter Brown, *Augustine of Hippo: A Biography*, rev. ed. (Berkeley: University of California Press, 2000), 201–6.

it were intermingle with each other, if human beings learned nothing from other humans.[23]

For Augustine, questions of social context, sermon form, presentation, the role of imagination, and the use of stories and illustrations are critically important. But they are secondary to the discipline of reading Scripture in the church; and more so, they spring out of it. Augustine knew about the erosion of confidence in Scripture. He too said that we are not good at reading Scripture. Why? In part because we are not good at seeing this truth: what is written in the Scriptures is better and truer—even if its meaning is hidden—than anything we could think of by ourselves.[24]

Augustine was a pastor and understood that he was bound both to the people God had entrusted to his care and to God's Word. He assigns a privileged place not only to Scripture but also to the community of the church. In its creeds, liturgies, and rule of faith, the church is the corporate memory of the one Scripture points to and reveals. In all these, the church turns toward Christ, head of the broken body, and toward its neighbor. Thus, to interpret Scripture is not an end in itself but a part of the life of holiness. The interpretation of Scripture means nothing if it does not build up the body of Christ. Augustine states this rule for interpreting Scripture at the end of book 1 of *On Christian Teaching*: "So anyone who thinks that he has understood the divine scriptures or any part of them, but cannot by his understanding build up this double love of God and neighbor, has not yet succeeded in understanding them."[25] Augustine understood that his vocations to teach, preach, and love his people were intertwined: they were a single calling.

To Look Again Rather Than Elsewhere

In response to the Western erosion of confidence in the gospel, we do not need to walk out of Scripture's room into order to preach sermons that are good news to our people. God comes to us in what is weak and

---

23. Augustine, preface to *On Christian Teaching* 1:13–14, pp. 5–6.
24. Kolbet, *Augustine and the Cure of Souls*, 142.
25. Augustine, *On Christian Teaching* 1.86.

rejected, especially in the strange words of Scripture, in order to give us life in his Son. The Spirit guides us to look again at Scripture and the church, attentively, obediently, and expectantly, rather than looking elsewhere. To attend to it with a guide for its navigation is far less of a burden on the preacher than trying to erect one rickety bridge of meaning after another. Relevance is not established by connecting the text with objective truths or doctrine; with the expectations, perceptions, and felt needs of the hearers; or with some universal experience. It is established by inviting hearers to join you, the preacher, as you stand under the Word—the same Word that addresses Israel, Mary, Paul, the Corinthians, believers across the ages, and the contemporary church. I hope these Six Questions will help us discover how to do just that—to know what to do with what we see and hear.

1

"What Do I See?"

The Preacher as Witness

▶ **Main action:** Attentively read the appointed Scriptures.

We begin with attentiveness to the text—slow, patient reading—with the knowledge that this is a spiritual practice through which God molds and shapes the preacher. We begin with attentiveness characterized by deference to what we see in Scripture, even when it offends, confuses, or seems a dead letter. This is the role of the preacher as witness. Could we, with Augustine, understand that the slow, attentive reading of Scripture is meant to develop our weak perceptive powers to see that what is written in the Scriptures is better and truer—even if its meaning is hidden—than anything we could think of by ourselves?[1] We proceed with this hope.

Attentiveness as Divine Remedy in a Postmodern World

In and of itself, attentive reading is a divine gift to a world of constructed realities, well barricaded against assaults. And not only our world.

---

1. Kolbet, *Augustine and the Cure of Souls,* 142.

Augustine criticized the Stoics' dependence on their own virtues. Why? Because it closed them off to a world beyond their carefully constructed selves.[2] Paul Kolbet, in his retrieval of Augustine's classical idea of the cure of the soul, aptly writes, "The world of signification we live in today is one where we are impatient with signification that does not refer to ourselves."[3]

In August 2014, a subcommittee of the Committee on Academic Freedom and Tenure of the American Association of University Professors wrote a report on their response to the growing demand for trigger warnings on university syllabi. They wrote:

> A current threat to academic freedom in the classroom comes from a demand that teachers provide warnings in advance if assigned material contains anything that might trigger difficult emotional responses for students. This follows from earlier calls not to offend students' sensibilities by introducing material that challenges their values and beliefs. The specific call for "trigger warnings" began in the blogosphere as a caution about graphic descriptions of rape on feminist sites, and has now migrated to university campuses in the form of requirements or proposals that students be alerted to all manner of topics that some believe may deeply offend and even set off a post-traumatic stress disorder (PTSD) response in some individuals. Oberlin College's original policy (since tabled to allow for further debate in the face of faculty opposition) is an example of the range of possible trigger topics: "racism, classism, sexism, heterosexism, cissexism, ableism, and other issues of privilege and oppression." It went on to say that a novel like Chinua Achebe's *Things Fall Apart* might "trigger readers who have experienced racism, colonialism, religious persecution, violence, suicide and more." It further cautioned faculty to "remove triggering material when it does not contribute directly to the course learning goals."[4]

The debate about trigger warnings has triggered (!) an extensive conversation about the purpose of education, the role of texts in classrooms, the mental health of university students, and most importantly

---

2. Kolbet, *Augustine and the Cure of Souls*, 195.
3. Kolbet, *Augustine and the Cure of Souls*, 186.
4. "On Trigger Warnings," American Association of University Professors, August 2014, https://www.aaup.org/report/trigger-warnings.

how to make college campuses safer places. Central to the conversation about trigger warnings is the question of the educational role of looking attentively at difficult texts. A *New Republic* article on the subject was accompanied by a picture of a young white woman wearing a blindfold.[5] Must we look away from that which offends, challenges, upsets? Is exposure to any sort of "ism" a form of violence? How do we distinguish between that which is offensive and that which can cause trauma? Who decides?

Listening to God's address is hard at the best of times. Eli and Samuel tell us at least this. If it were easy, the church would not have developed the discipline of *lectio divina*, and Thomas Cranmer would not have created a structure of morning and evening prayer to protect the reading and hearing of "the very pure Word of God, the holy Scriptures."[6] But when Scripture offends? The church, of course, has already exercised its own form of trigger warnings, with the exclusion of difficult texts or portions of psalms left out of the Revised Common Lectionary and the Common Lectionary before that. Pastors who select their own weekly or daily Scripture are not exempt from this practice of excising portions of Scripture they deem unsavory. Selecting a single passage on which to hang a whole worship service or lifting up a theme well above Scripture's thick jungle does not serve the spiritual practice of attentiveness as a divine gift.

What is lost with this trend is both the practice of reading difficult texts and the practice of listening to them and preaching from them. To look away is to shut a door on the Spirit as it enters our small worlds. As I noted in the introduction, Augustine writes of the discipline we must develop in order to stay with the difficult parts of Scripture. The skills we need to read Scripture properly are the very ones needed to act morally.

5. For a discussion of trigger warnings, see Greg Lukianoff and Jonathan Haidt, "The Coddling of the American Mind," *The Atlantic*, September 2015, https://www.theatlantic .com/magazine/archive/2015/09/the-coddling-of-the-american-mind/399356/. For the referenced image and more on trigger warnings in the classroom, see Jennie Jarvie, "Trigger Happy," *New Republic*, March 3, 2014, https://newrepublic.com/article/116842 /trigger-warnings-have-spread-blogs-college-classes-thats-bad.

6. "Nothing is ordained to be read, but the very pure Word of God, the holy Scriptures, or that which is agreeable to the same; and that in such a Language and Order as is most easy and plain for the understanding both of the Readers and Hearers." See the preface (1886) to the *Book of Common Prayer*, reprinted in *Book of Common Prayer* (Toronto: Anglican Book Centre, 1962), 715.

Here is a divine remedy for a postmodern world. The art of attentively reading the strange, sometimes difficult words of Scripture is similar to the ability to love our neighbor across the chasm of difference and offense.

In the context of eroding skills and declining openness to hearing the strange voice of Scripture, the church claims to be a community poised to hear God's voice. The fact that the task of listening to God's address is situated within a community, in and of itself, as Augustine says, speaks of the social nature of sin and grace. He observed that Adam's sin had to do with his joining a community that was turned toward itself, cordoned off from God. At its most basic level, the church functions as a community for hearing—albeit imperfectly and often not at all—because it is turned *outward* toward Christ and its neighbor.[7]

Scripture as Fixed Text and Discourse

Scripture is a fixed, written text. Though we take this for granted, this fact allows God's Word to endure across cultures, continents, and centuries. Because it is a fixed text and canon (in many translations), we read basically the same words in Brooklyn in 2016 as were read in Bombay in 1614 and in North Africa in 314. Scripture is also more than a written text. It is discourse, address, interpretation, inspiration, and proclamation in gloriously varied ways. To explore how the Spirit uses Scripture to build the church by creating a people able to respond to it, we must first distinguish Scripture as fixed text and discourse. Scripture displays characteristics both of written texts, consistent across time, and of things said, utterances, which will be read and pondered in ways that are not fully fixed.[8]

Both characteristics of Scripture—as fixed text and as discourse—allow it "to intrude on the church" as the one witness of the one Spirit, and allow it to be read, heard, preached, pondered, received, and embodied across time and contexts.[9] To describe Scripture as only the construction of the church over the centuries is to collapse the distinction between what the text says and what the interpreter or interpretive

7. Kolbet, *Augustine and the Cure of Souls*, 132.
8. Yeago, "Bible: The Spirit, the Church and the Scriptures," 49–93.
9. Yeago, "Bible: The Spirit, the Church and the Scriptures," 63.

community makes of the text. The church is committed to the belief that Scripture has been received from the prophets and apostles, and the church does not in any simple sense construct it. This allows the Spirit freedom and authority to intrude on us through the otherness of the text. To say that the Spirit uses Scripture to create a people able to respond to it is to speak of the Spirit putting the fixed texts to work sacramentally. The Spirit takes up the fixed texts and gathers them into a single discourse addressed to the church. In doing so, the Spirit renders human discourse as divine discourse.[10]

We begin the Six Questions with attentiveness to the written text because the written text is the main material of Scripture. To begin here in our role as witness means we pay attention to how the words form sentences and how the sentences connect to each other. In his book *How to Write a Sentence: And How to Read One*, Stanley Fish retells a story from Annie Dillard's *The Writing Life* (1989):

> Annie Dillard tells of a fellow writer who was asked by a student, "Do you think I could be a writer?" "Well," the writer said, "do you like sentences?" The student was surprised by the question, but Dillard knows exactly what was meant. He was being told, she explains, that "if he liked sentences he could begin," and she remembers a similar conversation with a painter friend. "I asked him how he came to be a painter. He said, 'I like the smell of paint.'"

As Fish writes, the implicit point is that "you don't begin with a grand conception, either of the great American novel or a masterpiece that will hang in the Louvre"—or of how you will preach on a particular text. You begin with "a feel for the nitty-gritty material of the medium, paint in one case, sentences in the other."[11]

Deferential Attention to the Text

What does it mean to have "deferential attention" to the text? Toward what should our deference be directed? First, we defer to Scripture's words and sentences, including the difficult parts. We do not look away,

10. Yeago, "Bible: The Spirit, the Church and the Scriptures," 63.
11. Stanley Fish, *How to Write a Sentence: And How to Read One* (New York: HarperCollins, 2011), 1.

skip, or gloss over. We pay attention to the nouns that are the subject of its verbs. We pay attention to what the text says, not what we think it says or what we want it to say. We do not extrapolate its meaning or teaching and then discard its words, sentences, and narrative. We take the actual words of Scripture seriously, all of them, even when they grate and hurt, as words intended by God for us on whom the end of the ages has come. We pay careful attention to what Scripture says and how the words work together in the text.

This simple practice needs to be emphasized. Paying attention to sentences—nouns, verbs, and direct objects—leads the preacher to identify the active agent in a sentence and, hopefully, to reflect this in her sermons. Let me give you an example. I recently heard a sermon on the parable of the weeds among the wheat (Matt. 13:24–30, 36–43), assigned in the Revised Common Lectionary, Year A, during the long season of Pentecost (the seventh Sunday after Pentecost). A fertile image for the height of summer. The sermon encouraged the congregation to "sow seeds of love," and the preacher passed out packets of flower seeds printed with these words to emphasize the message. The focus of the sermon was on our actions, not God's or the evil one's. It was well-meaning, but what it lacked was a reflection on what the passage actually says through its nouns and verbs. In contrast to the sermon, the active agents in this story (the subject of its sentences) are the householder or the Son of Man (vv. 27, 30, 37, 41), the enemy or the devil (vv. 25, 39), and the reapers or angels whom the Son of Man instructs to gather the wheat and burn the weeds at harvest time (vv. 30, 41). The *only* action assigned to the congregation comes through the command to listen: "Let anyone with ears listen!" (v. 43). What might the congregation have heard if the sermon reflected an attentiveness to the text?

Second, we read Scripture in light of how the church has interpreted it through the ages. This does not mean our response is static or uncritical, liberal or conservative, per se. It does mean that we do not come up with our own personal interpretation of Scripture that casually ignores or contradicts how the church has understood Scripture's meaning through the centuries. We do not read Scripture as primarily about the individual believer and personal piety. Rather, it is about God and Jesus Christ, the corporate community of God's people, Israel and the church, and our role in God's mission in Christ through the Spirit.

Finally, to defer to the text means we defer to Jesus Christ, who is revealed there and who is the active agent in many of Scripture's sentences. Scripture is not a symbolic language that points to a universal human experience; nor is it a textbook on doctrine or an instruction book on how to lead a moral life. It is not a text we stand outside of to analyze or master. It is not something to be managed with our skills and certainly not within our sermon preparation. It is God's living Word, which through the Spirit blows where it will and intrudes, claims, judges, and brings to life that which is not. It is about the God who created this world, what has happened to that world, and what God has done and is doing to redeem it and set it right through his ascended Son, Jesus Christ. All of Scripture points to Jesus Christ, Son of the God of Israel, who drew the whole world to himself on the cross. To defer to the text means we allow ourselves, the church, and the world to be read by it, addressed by it, and over time re-formed into the image of the one who has claimed us in his Word, Jesus Christ.

Tools for Deferential Attentiveness

In the Denver Art Museum, the curators and educators have created educational kits for parents and children to use as they wander through the paintings, photographs, artifacts, or sculptures in the museum's galleries. These kits come either in backpacks or in long tubes. Out of them children pull various aids to help them look at the art and explore the relationships between the paintings, photographs, artifacts, or sculptures that the curators have brought together into an exhibit. They might pull out games, mosaic tiles, feathers, felt hats, reproductions, 3-D glasses, quizzes, or stories. In the Western American exhibit visitors can make their own postcards using the colors of the western landscape. In the drawing studio, pencils and easels are set out for use. Visit the museum and you will see children and adults sitting on the floor or at low tables, surrounded by beautiful art, looking, gazing, comparing, drawing, coloring, dressing up, and most important of all, lingering. Few children—or parents—are running for the exit.

For each of the Six Questions of the Sermon, the suggested practices are intended to be like the educational kits in the Denver Art Museum. Not feathers or 3-D glasses but heuristic questions and directives, designed to help preachers linger and look at the beauty in Scripture and the relationships between its texts, creatively engaging it longer than they might otherwise have done. The goal is to aid and encourage attentive looking and listening, knowing that the preacher needs to do something with what she sees and hears. She has a sermon to preach. The hope is to prevent preachers from leaving Scripture's room too quickly and stepping outside it in order to preach it.

Here are six tools for the first question of sermon preparation, What do I see? Additional directions accompany each tool or guideline to help the preacher read attentively.

1. Read slowly and attentively.
   a. Do not try to mine it for meaning or a sermon idea at this point.
   b. Sit with it passively until it yields its treasures.
   c. Notice what offends you or makes you uncomfortable.
2. Focus on the movement of the passage.
   a. Pay attention to nouns, verbs, and direct objects. Who is the active agent in a sentence or passage?
   b. Consider the movement within each sentence (word by word or phrase by phrase) or within the passage (sentence by sentence) of an epistle, prose section, psalm, or other piece of poetry.
   c. Consider the canonical movement from one piece of Scripture (word, image, action, phrase, etc.) to echoes elsewhere.
3. Read around.
   a. Read all the Scripture appointed for the day along with surrounding chapters.
   b. If the passage is a New Testament text, read parallel passages and Old Testament references.
   c. Read intratextually and figurally.[12] Follow images, references, descriptions, and citations from one part of Scripture to another, back and forth between the New and Old Testaments.

---

12. For definition and explanation see the next section, "Reading around the Scriptures."

4. Read through the eyes of your congregation.[13]

    a. What are the cultures and subcultures of your congregation?

    b. Consider what they would notice that you might not.

    c. How do they see themselves in relationship to the world?

5. Do your homework.

    a. Know the basic historical-critical situation. Look up terms, people, or situations you don't know or understand.

    b. Study important Greek or Hebrew words. Read in the original language if you can.

    c. Use trustworthy theological commentaries and biblical tools.

6. Identify God's activity in the passage.

    a. What is God doing or how is God acting in the passage? Is God making, keeping, or fulfilling a promise? Is God suffering, displaying power through a miracle, displaying judgment, or acting in mercy, provision, or patience? Is Jesus teaching the disciples, praying, or exhorting?

    b. What does the order of words in a sentence or the progression of thoughts in an argument describe about the divine-human relationship? About God and Israel? God and the church? God and sin? God and the follower? God and the wanderer? God and the future?

Reading around the Scriptures: Intratextual and Figural Interpretation for Preaching Jesus Christ

In my previous church, each of the Sunday school classrooms for younger children had a sand table. These were large, flat boxes, with edges tall enough to hold in the sand but low enough so children could easily reach in to play. On the shelves of the classroom were wooden figures of the main characters in Scripture, as well as a little altar, a church, rocks, miniature trees, cars, birds, and all kinds of plastic animals. When you added in the toys the children brought to class,

13. See chap. 3 of Lenora Tubbs Tisdale, *Preaching as Local Theology and Folk Art* (Minneapolis: Fortress, 1997) for an extensive guide to exegeting one's congregation for preaching.

the Sunday school rooms ended up with quite a menagerie. The class began as children and teachers lit the Christ candle and prayed together. Then the children would play at the sand table. Sarah and Abraham would be in the desert along with Jesus, a favorite action figure, a toy dinosaur, and a few shepherds or kings from the classroom nativity set. Together they would all march through the wilderness until they had bread and wine next to Jesus and the Hello Kitty figure that one child had put in the middle of the sand.

No one told these children this isn't how it happened. That it was Moses and Miriam, not Abraham and Sarah, who marched through the desert of Egypt, that Jesus and the shepherds were born long after the wilderness wanderings, and that action figures hadn't been invented yet. The teachers knew not to tell them, and so they didn't. It never occurred to the children to do anything other than what they did: take the figures and stories of Scripture, the things they love, and mix them up in a single world.

An attentive reading of Scripture includes learning to read it in a way similar to how these children play. That is, we must play around in it, trusting that the Scriptures of the Old and New Testaments are a single witness to God. An attentive reading includes exploring how one story, figure, or image leads to another, back and forth across the Testaments, beyond the limits of a historical-critical reading and the immediate referent for a given story, figure, or image. This kind of play teaches us to trust that God is opening up the Scripture to us, and, most importantly, us to it. It teaches us to be less worried about what Scripture means exactly so we might be open to what it does. As our lives and our congregations are drawn into it, God creates a single world.

A "theological reading" of Scripture refers to a cluster of interpretative methods, each of which privileges the theological nature of Scripture and its message. John Webster defines theological reading as "interpretation informed by a theological description of the nature of the biblical writings and their reception, setting them in the scope of the progress of the saving divine Word through time."[14]

---

14. John Webster, *Domain of the Word: Scripture and Theological Reason* (New York: T&T Clark, 2012), 30. Reading Scripture intratextually comes out of the work of George Lindbeck, based in part on the work of Hans Frei, Clifford Geertz, and Erich Auerbach. The entire canon of the Old and New Testament is read as "a canonically and narrationally

To read around in it, across the Testaments, is to speak of two central approaches to a theological reading: intratextual reading and figural reading. Both an intratextual and a figural reading of Scripture locate the meaning of Scripture within Scripture itself (intra) rather than outside it (extra) or in truths, doctrines, or (a shared) human experience. Both intertextual and intratextual approaches to Scripture insist that the meaningful referents of Scripture are found within other parts of the scriptural text and hence that the interpretation of biblical texts is to be measured by other biblical texts. Those who use the term "intratextual" in this case are thinking of Scripture as one single and integrated text, while those who use the term "intertextual" are thinking of Scripture as a collection of discrete texts, which are nonetheless to be read together and in light of one another. However, because the Scriptures are God's own creative word, the meaning found within them is not limited to the world of Scripture. That meaning refers and extends to all worlds, including our own, because all worlds and all times are of God's creation and redemption.

An intratextual reading invites the preacher to move around in and back and forth between texts and Testaments. The biblical scholar Beth LaNeel Tanner, using the related term "intertextuality,"[15] describes this movement: "The intertextual reader-writer does not always look for a fixed meaning of a word or phrase, but for a more fluid possibility. The intertextual reader-writer is always looking for how a text refers to other 'texts,' sometimes as a simile, sometimes as a parody, sometimes as a presupposition. The intertextual reader-writer uses other texts to say more than is apparent in the printed text—words and even worlds

---

unified and internally glossed (that is, self-referential and self-integrating) whole centered on Jesus Christ, and telling the story of the dealings of the Triune God with his people and his world in ways which are typologically applicable to the present." See Lindbeck, *Church in a Postliberal Age*, 203.

15. Tanner speaks of intertextual reading as contrasted with intratextual. While distinct, the movement she describes in this quotation is the same. Intertextual reading is a literary term. For a succinct overview see Stephen Heath, "Intertextuality," in *A Dictionary of Cultural and Critical Theory*, ed. Michael Payne (Oxford, UK: Blackwell, 1996), 258–59. The term refers to the complex relationship between literary texts as a means of communication. To read Scripture intertextually would be to view it as a set of multiple texts. To read it intratextually is to read it as a single text. See Richard B. Hays, Stefan Alkier, and Leroy A. Huizenga, eds., *Reading the Bible Intertextually* (Waco: Baylor University Press, 2009).

hidden between the lines, and meanings are formed from a variety of spheres of reference."[16]

"Figural reading" is a term that describes a particular way to order and interpret this more general intratextual movement, and it derives from a more particular theological understanding of how the biblical text "works." It is based on a knowledge that in Scripture a given image, person, city, or story has more than one referent and that these referents are linked in a certain way. Thus, figural reading both opens up and limits how the preacher connects the two Testaments through specific texts in each.

A central form of this connection is typology. The New Testament teaches that there are types and shadows in the Old Testament (Rom. 5:14; Heb. 8:5). These various types and shadows find their fulfillment in Jesus Christ. Jesus is the "antitype," that is, the fulfillment of all that comes before him. Reading Scripture typologically is based on God's sovereign ordering of Scripture. Theologian Richard Lints describes this ordering of Scripture through time. "While the type does have significance for its own time, its greater significance is directed toward the future. It testifies to something greater than itself that is yet to come. The future antitype will surely come, because God will providentially bring it to pass. It is God's ability to hold history together that serves as the foundation of typology."[17]

How might one read Scripture for sermon preparation using intratextual reading and figural reading? Although I treat these two approaches separately, as hermeneutically distinct, they are in fact two sides of the same theological coin.[18] Both take as their starting point

16. Beth LaNeel Tanner, *The Book of Psalms through the Lens of Intertextuality*, Studies in Biblical Literature 26 (New York: Peter Lang, 2001), 50.

17. Richard Lints, *The Fabric of Theology: A Prolegomenon to Evangelical Theology* (Grand Rapids: Eerdmans, 1993), 306.

18. More specifically, George Lindbeck provides a particular description of this scriptural "nature" and presses for the development of the practice of reading Scripture intratextually. To read intratextually is to "redescribe reality within the scriptural framework rather than translating scripture into categories extra scriptural" (*Church in a Postliberal Age*, 118). Figural reading stands as a specific kind of intratextual interpretation and harks back to patristic practice. Hans Frei, in *The Eclipse of Biblical Narrative* (New Haven: Yale University Press, 1974), demonstrates that reading Scripture as an interconnected unity was the practice of the church up until the eighteenth and nineteenth centuries. "Figural interpretation, then, sets forth the unity of the canon as a single cumulative pattern of meaning" (33–34). In figural reading, Scripture is taken by

the theological claim that all of Scripture is a single witness to God and to God's single mission across all ages, culminating in Jesus Christ, the Son of the God of Israel. Within the sweep of Scripture's time—its stories, nations, and peoples—we can see the arc of God's singular movement across all time, including our own. This movement draws all things together in Christ, who "is before all things, and in [whom] all things hold together" (Col. 1:17).

Our hope is that the Holy Spirit uses our preaching of Scripture as an instrument of this ordering. As we are drawn into the reality of God's singular movement, we come to know ourselves, our churches, and our worlds as part of this ordering.

Scripture as a Single Witness

This theological claim, that the Spirit uses all of Scripture as a single witness to Jesus Christ, invites the preacher to critically engage Scripture intratextually and figurally. Each text is a doorway, window, passage, or rabbit hole into Scripture's full witness to Jesus Christ. Thomas Breidenthal describes the canon as "a vast hologram":

> God's truth is present in Scripture the way it is present in any genuine witness; it descends to meet it and fill it in its upward movement. For this reason every word, every nuance of diction and sequence, is saturated and overflowing with God's word. The canon of Scripture is like a vast hologram, each portion of which contains the whole message of creation, judgment, redemption, and call. If the witness is true, then what the witness points to is contained therein.[19]

A return to an intratextual and a figural reading of Scripture is part of a theological interpretation of Scripture that is now being

---

the interpreter as a series of referents within the text, which draw us as readers to other referents within the Bible, across time and space, however these may be constituted. As readers are drawn into this cross-referencing, they are also drawn into the actual living world of Scripture's own reality.

19. Thomas Breidenthal, "Sharper Than a Two-Edged Sword: Following the Logic of the Text in Preaching," in *Sharper Than a Two-Edged Sword: Preaching, Teaching and Living the Bible*, ed. Michael Root and James J. Buckley (Grand Rapids: Eerdmans, 2008), 35. See also Kevin J. Vanhoozer, ed., *Dictionary for Theological Interpretation of the Bible* (Grand Rapids: Baker Academic, 2005).

retrieved, reengaged, and explored across the church. For example, in a figural reading, the divided Israel of the books of Kings also refers to the divided church, and theologians have made use of this linkage in rich and challenging ways.[20] In the eucharistic liturgy the church holds up a theological (intratextual and figural) reading of Scripture when, for instance, the minister breaks the blessed communion bread and proclaims, "Alleluia, Christ our Passover has been sacrificed for us" (cf. 1 Cor. 5:7). This kind of figural reading in the liturgy has deep roots in the Christian tradition, including in the Scriptures themselves.

Reading Scripture as a single witness to Jesus Christ has been the norm for most of church history.[21] Scripture itself presents this single witness as the way the resurrected Jesus teaches the disciples to read it. On the road to Emmaus, when the risen Christ joins the two disciples who are walking away from Jerusalem, they are kept from recognizing him (Luke 24:13–35). What does Jesus do to aid recognition? Earlier that morning he called Mary by name so that she might recognize him, and she does, saying, "Rabbouni!" (John 20:16). But this isn't

20. See, for example, George Lindbeck, "The Church as Israel: Ecclesiology and Ecumenism," in *Jews and Christians: People of God*, ed. Carl E. Braaten and Robert W. Jenson (Grand Rapids: Eerdmans, 2003), 78–94.

21. Frei, *Eclipse of Biblical Narrative*. The theological claim that Scripture is a single testimony to Jesus Christ is a claim about the nature of Scripture and the nature of God. It can also be construed as a claim about the role of the preacher: the preacher is a witness to Jesus Christ. In 1997 Charles Campbell, in *Preaching Jesus*, developed an approach to preaching based on the claim that all of Scripture is a single witness to Jesus Christ. Based on the work of Hans Frei of the Yale School of postliberal theology, Campbell called for sermons that use the ascriptive logic of Scripture as their guide. Scripture's ascriptive logic, according to Frei, is that the identity of Jesus Christ, revealed in the events of Scripture, is not symbolic, arbitrary, or one of many possibilities. Another version of Jesus Christ cannot be substituted for the identity revealed in Scripture. Frei also uses the phrase "the unsubstitutable identity of Jesus Christ," meaning that Jesus's identity can be no other than what is revealed in Scripture, which is unique to him. Jesus is the true, living God. Scripture, and thus our sermons, is primarily about God. See Hans Frei, *The Identity of Jesus Christ: The Hermeneutic Bases of Dogmatic Theology* (Philadelphia: Fortress, 1975), 102–6. Campbell describes faithful preaching as an interpretive performance of the story of Jesus on behalf of the church. The role of the preacher is to "dare to preach Jesus of Nazareth in all his particularity by rendering him as the subject of his own predicates." Charles Campbell, *Preaching Jesus: New Directions for Homiletics in Hans Frei's Postliberal Theology* (Grand Rapids: Eerdmans, 1997), 193.

what Jesus does here. Instead, as they walk along the road, he reads and interprets Scripture with them. Luke writes, "Then beginning with Moses and all the prophets, he interpreted to them the things about himself in all the scriptures" (Luke 24:27).

Likewise, when the risen Christ comes among his disciples that same evening, what does he do? He says, "Peace be with you"; he shows them the wounds in his flesh; he eats broiled fish in their presence; and then, again, he reads and interprets Scripture with them. He "open[s] their minds" to understand that "everything written about [him] in the law of Moses, the prophets, and the psalms must be fulfilled" (Luke 24:44–46).

The Logic behind an Intratextual and a Figural Reading of Scripture

Reading Scripture intratextually, unlike the children's play in the sand table during Sunday school, does not mean that anything goes. Perhaps it is helpful to think of Scripture as a symphony, to borrow an idea from Hans Urs von Balthasar's *Truth Is Symphonic*.[22] Each movement has its own leitmotif, each instrument its own role; and through the symphony they speak back and forth, repeat themes, pick them up, play off each other, and in doing so create a single coherent thing of beauty.

Scripture's internal logic, its intratextuality, is not based on chord structure, key signatures, or rhythm—or the extent of the preacher's imagination. Its internal logic is based on God's unity and purpose for creation, which is to make all things one in Christ (Eph. 1:10). In sermon preparation, this theological claim guides our reading, what we look for, and where it leads. We don't "play around" in Scripture simply to exercise our imaginations or creativity. We read intratextually and figurally because doing so reveals the full depth of God's unifying purposes in Jesus Christ across the centuries and continents. We read Scripture as an expression of this unity and, more than an expression, as an instrument of that unity in the Spirit's hands. As we open up and are drawn into Scripture, this unifying Spirit presses on the church, creating and re-creating it.

22. Hans Urs von Balthasar, *Truth Is Symphonic: Aspects of Christian Pluralism*, trans. Graham Harrison (San Francisco: Ignatius, 1987).

An Intratextual Reading

Using the story of the rich man and the parable of the wedding guest, I will give an example of an intratextual reading of Scripture for sermon preparation. I will continue with this example in the following section as I turn to a figural reading of Scripture.

In reading the story of Jesus and the rich man (Matt. 19:16–26; Mark 10:17–27; Luke 18:18–30), many readers are struck by the man's silence in response to Jesus's command to sell his possessions and give the money to the poor (Mark 10:21). This is clear in all three accounts. The man could have responded to Jesus in several ways. He could have asked Jesus for help, for mercy. He could have repented of his love of possessions. He could have complained that this was too hard (as Moses complained in the wilderness). When the rich man fails to respond, Jesus turns to his disciples and makes a statement about his ability to help the rich man: "For God all things are possible" (Matt. 19:26; Mark 10:27). Jesus's statement about God's power in the face of human weakness can increase the reader's wonder about the rich man's silence. Here is an individual standing face-to-face with Jesus, with whom all things are possible, and the man asks for nothing. Silence is his response to the presence, power, and mercy of God.

Reading this story intratextually opens a door into the silence of the poorly clothed wedding guest (Matt. 22:1–14; Luke 14:16–24). In Matthew's Gospel this story is in close proximity to the story of the rich man. In this parable the king asks the lonely guest, "Friend, how did you get in here without a wedding robe?" In response the guest is speechless (Matt. 22:12). As with the rich man, the wedding guest could have responded in several ways. He could have said, "You invited me in," or "your generosity is how I got in," or "I know I'm not properly dressed, but please let me stay." In moving from the silent rich man to the speechless wedding guest, Scripture invites the preacher to reflect on human silence in response to God, as God addresses us and waits for our response. Is our silence an unwillingness to respond to God? Is it fear or shame? An inability to speak of or ask for God's mercy and grace?

At this point the preacher can continue with an intratextual reading of these Scriptures by moving in two directions. She can look for other examples of silence as an inability or unwillingness to respond to God's presence and address, be it in individuals, families, Israel, or the church. In Isaiah, God repeatedly describes Israel's iniquity in terms of their silence in response to his call. "Why, when I called, was there no one to answer?" (50:2; see also Isa. 65:12; 66:4; Jer. 7:13, 27). Or she can look for contrasting images. The preacher could turn to the story of the blind men calling for Jesus as he leaves Jericho. The crowds rebuke them, "telling them to be silent." The blind men respond by crying out all the more, "Have mercy on us, Son of David" (Matt. 20:29–34; Luke 18:35–42). The blind men's refusal to keep silent can lead the preacher to consider what Jesus says as he travels from the Mount of Olives toward Jerusalem. Some of the Sanhedrin in the crowd order Jesus to silence the "whole multitude of the disciples" who are loudly praising God "for all the deeds of power that they [have] seen." Jesus says, "I tell you, if these were silent, the stones would shout out" (Luke 19:37–40). An intratextual reading of the story of the rich man will thus open the preacher to multiple connections between scriptural texts, in this case related to God's address and call to individuals, Israel, and the church, and their unwillingness or inability to respond, which takes the form of silence.

A Figural Reading: The Speechless Wedding Guest and the Silent Lamb Led to Slaughter

Intratextual readings open the preacher to similarities, echoes, or thematic connections between diverse texts. A figural reading goes further and attributes these connections to a divine intentionality: a given text actually *means* more than one thing. In fact, it "means" or refers to other texts quite explicitly. Thus, to say that scriptural texts can have multiple referents is to say that they speak to each other back and forth across and beyond the Testaments—based on images, themes, patterns, and echoes—and that they do so for a divine purpose. For example, in Exodus 12, the roasted lamb the Israelites were instructed to eat hastily, with their sandals tied and belts fastened, refers not only to the first Passover meal but also to Jesus Christ. John the Baptist proclaims in John 1:29, "Here is the Lamb of God who takes away the sin of the world!" In this case, these connections were viewed by the New Testament authors not as personally imaginative construals but as actual meanings that were rooted in the original text of the Old Testament.

A figural reading of the story of the rich man would take his silence as a textually deliberate opening to truths disclosed or referred to in other parts of Scripture. Hence, we can interpret the silence of the rich man, the wedding guest, and Israel based on Scripture's internal logic: to make all things one in Christ. The preacher turns to the suffering servant, who did not open his mouth as he was led to slaughter (Isa. 53:7), and to Christ, who will not give an answer "even to a single charge" made against him (Matt. 27:14). Four times Jesus kept silent during his trial: before the Sanhedrin (Mark 14:60, 61), before Pilate (Mark 15:4–5), before Herod (Luke 23:9), and before Pilate a second time (John 19:9). What is the relationship between the silence of the wedding guest and the rich man, and the silence of Christ and the suffering servant? Here the preacher thinks figurally, remembering that Christ's silence has more than one referent. Christ's silence refers to his posture at his trial. Could it also refer to the silence of the wedding guest and the rich man? That is, could Christ's silence before Pilate embody a form of our inability or unwillingness to respond to God, or to ask for help, mercy, or forgiveness? Here the preacher is invited to see Christ's silence during questioning as one way Christ becomes our sin (2 Cor. 5:21). Christ is the fulfillment—what is traditionally called the "antitype"—of our unwillingness or inability to respond to God's call. Christ is the original form of Israel, among whom, as Isaiah said, when God called there was no one to answer. Christ is the fulfillment of all the silences that come before and after because he takes on our silence, our inability to ask for mercy, for help, for forgiveness. Christ takes on our unwillingness to commend others to God and to speak out against injustice. Christ is the wedding guest, Israel, the rich man, the church, and you and me in our inability to repent, to seek mercy, to praise God, or to speak prophetically. He becomes our silence and rises from the dead and speaks God's living Word. We are not left alone in our many silences because Christ comes so that our silences can be redeemed. All our silences find their fulfillment in Christ's. Because of God's actions in Christ, Christ can say, when the crowds ask him to silence his disciples, "I tell you, if these were silent, the stones would shout out" (Luke 19:40). Hence, to follow the traditional Christian approach to figural interpretation, the rich man's silence in the form of incapacity, and perhaps sin, turns out to be the "type" or shadow pointing forward to Christ's own redemptive silence.

Here is the beginning of a sermon. The goal is to draw one's congregation into Scripture's descriptions of silence as our personal and corporate inability or unwillingness to respond to God; after this, it is to draw the congregation into Scripture's description of Christ's own contrasting redemptive response. In doing so the preacher draws the congregation toward Christ as the one who calls and addresses us and redeems our inability and unwillingness to respond. The preacher invites her community (and herself) to see their own silence (and the church's) through the lens of Christ's actions. The focus could be our participation in Christ's redemption of our silence.[23] "Through him, then, let us continually offer a sacrifice of praise to God, that is, the fruit of lips that confess his name" (Heb. 13:15). A preacher could take the sermon in different directions, depending on her congregation and context, but always helping the congregation to recognize what it looks like to participate in Christ's redemption of our silence, as a congregation and as individuals.

What does a sermon based on an intratextual and figural reading of Scripture look like in the twenty-first century? Homileticians and theologians are only just beginning to explore this question.[24] It is not a method that, if rigorously applied, necessarily leads to singularly right answers about God and the world. Some figural readings can seem forced or end up falling flat. But even in these cases, to read figurally constitutes a deferential attention to the text and an openness to reading Scripture based on the kind of text it is in the Spirit's hands.

23. I offer the example from Acts 8:26–40. There the Ethiopian eunuch is reading the passage in Isaiah 53 about the silent lamb led to slaughter. Philip explains it to him with the good news of Jesus and, in contrast to the rich man and the wedding guest, his response is anything but silence. "As they were going along the road, they came to some water; and the eunuch said, 'Look, here is water! What is to prevent me from being baptized?' He commanded the chariot to stop, and both of them, Philip and the eunuch, went down into the water, and Philip baptized him" (Acts 8:36–38).

24. See sample sermons in Davis and Hays, *Art of Reading Scripture*, 277–325; Ephraim Radner, *Time and the Word: Figural Reading of the Christian Scriptures* (Grand Rapids: Eerdmans, 2016), 289–316.

The point of a sermon is not to show our work in some kind of tour de force or intricate calculation as if we were dutifully completing an algebra equation. It is to allow Scripture to become the lens through which we see our whole world as we move back and forth and forward in time. It is to find the right note in all our figural wonderings and use it as the place we travel with our congregations in our sermons. To preach from a figural reading of Scripture is to read and preach as one who witnesses to God, who in Scripture draws together and orders the whole world. We ourselves are creatures of such ordering. To open up Scripture in this way is to trust that in doing so, God will continue to open us up along with our congregations, so we may know ourselves, the church, and our many worlds as places of this divine ordering.

Preaching is well suited to this opening up of the self to the power Scripture has to order our lives. This divine ordering is the place God engages our thinking, our imagining, our vision. Any beloved and respected preacher might say in a sermon, "Imagine with me for a moment; imagine that we are like the . . ." This is an invitation to open up and be reshaped; and the congregation will follow.

What Do I See? The Preacher as Witness

To describe the preacher as a witness is to speak about stories and events. A witness testifies to something that has happened, whether it is a traffic accident or the resurrection. "It was a Monday morning and as I pulled out of the driveway, I saw . . ." The pastor's role as witness is certainly not limited to preaching. Pastors have the privilege of being invited into people's lives at the most important and intimate moments—when a tube must be removed from a loved one on life support or when a family receives news that their adoption is going through. We are called to create a safe space for our parishioners in our churches and offices so that they might honor us by asking, "Can I talk to you?" We know that if we sit, wait, and listen, they will tell us what has happened, the story or stories that have led them to seek us out. Members of our congregations, those we visit in jails or hospitals or those we talk to in coffee shops, do not tell us about abstract principles or moral exhortations in the raw. Love, justice, obedience, racism, redemption, and grace are always tied to events, to something that happened, to a story.

In this first of the Six Questions, the preacher begins sermon preparation as a witness to what she sees in Scripture, before she moves into the
practice of seeing Jesus Christ in Scripture's storied world and putting
herself in a position to be addressed by the one she sees. Attentiveness to
Scripture is both a spiritual practice and, as described in the introduction,
a divine remedy for the temptation to look away from what offends. The
Christian vocation of witness is by no means the province of preachers. It
is given to all followers by Christ. Just before his ascension, in response
to his disciples' questions about when he will restore the kingdom to
Israel, Jesus replies, "It is not for you to know the times or periods that
the Father has set by his own authority. But you will receive power when
the Holy Spirit has come upon you; and you will be my witnesses in Jerusalem, in all Judea and Samaria, and to the ends of the earth" (Acts 1:7–8).

All Christians are called to this life of witness and testimony. Anna
Carter Florence draws attention to this in *Preaching as Testimony*, and
Lillian Daniel writes of the experience of working with her congrega-
tion on this practice in *Tell It Like It Is*.[25] Marion Taylor and Agnes
Choi's book, *Handbook of Women Biblical Interpreters*, brings to light
the testimony of many unknown women.[26]

The preacher has a particular role as witness, however, which is tied
to the nature of Scripture's testimony. In his essay "The Hermeneutics
of Testimony," Paul Ricoeur explains the nature and function of this
testimony: First, the witness is sent in order to testify. Second, testimony comes from somewhere else and is about the global meaning of
human experience, which is God's own self. Third, testimony is oriented
toward proclamation. Fourth, testimony implies a total engagement of
persons, words, and acts to the point of sacrifice.[27] What distinguishes
the biblical use of testimony from its uses in ordinary language, Ricoeur
says, is that the testimony does not belong to the witness. "It proceeds
from an absolute initiative as to its origin and its content."[28]

25. Anna Carter Florence, *Preaching as Testimony* (Louisville: Westminster John Knox,
2007); Lillian Daniel, *Tell It Like It Is: Reclaiming the Practice of Testimony* (Lanham, MD:
Rowman & Littlefield, 2006).

26. Marion Taylor and Agnes Choi, *Handbook of Women Biblical Interpreters: A Historical
and Biographical Guide* (Grand Rapids: Baker Academic, 2012).

27. Paul Ricoeur, "The Hermeneutics of Testimony," in *Essays on Biblical Interpretation*,
ed. Lewis Mudge (Philadelphia: Fortress, 1980), 131–42.

28. Ricoeur, "Hermeneutics of Testimony," 131.

Thus, the preacher as witness begins with attentiveness to Scripture's detail, its nouns and verbs, hard parts and all. She testifies to what she has seen in the texts she has studied with deferential attention. She witnesses to the texts' movements, details, words, and sentences. The preacher cannot skip over them, ignore them, or leave them behind like husks once she has gleaned the meaning of a passage or story. To do so is to be something other than a witness. The details, events, and stories are essential. The absolute is always tied to narrated events.

The preacher will then move on from this first question and from her role as witness to what she has seen. She will move on to testify to the one she has seen and then, refusing to stand outside of her witness, to her own confession of the one she has testified about. But we ought to resist the urge to move there too quickly, knowing that deferential attentiveness to the fixed text of Scripture characterizes the preacher as witness and is the foundation of her role as confessor and theologian.

2

"Whom Do I See?"

The Preacher as Witness to Christ

▶ **Main action:** Describe the identity of Jesus Christ revealed in the text.

Years ago, I taught for a semester in a private Episcopal high school in New York City. I was filling in for a religious studies teacher who was on maternity leave. I took over her courses, her syllabi, and her ambivalent students, many of whom were from nominal Christian and Jewish homes. Most had never read the Old Testament or much of the New Testament. At the beginning of the term, they struggled with reading the Bible at all and struggled even more with finding a way to talk about what they were reading. "Why do we have to talk about God?" they complained. "This is a course on the Bible as literature," I replied, "and God is the main character."

After about six weeks of class I noticed a shift in the students' attitudes. They had begun to develop a vocabulary to talk about what they were reading: covenant, promises, the people of Israel, disciples, the church. I assigned the passion narratives late in the term. "Read all four and compare their narratives." One young woman came to class

41

with her homework completed and some urgent questions born out of the sense of injustice teenagers often feel so strongly. "Why didn't he fight back? Why didn't Jesus try to defend himself?"

She had never before read the story of Christ's trial, death, and resurrection. Never. Her sense of injustice was prompted by what she could see in the text that is lost to those of us who know this story well. Her response was a gift to me and to the students who had not noticed this consistent characterization of Jesus.

I could go on to describe what her observation of Jesus's unwilling-ness to fight back during his arrest, trial, and torture reveals about his identity.[1] Through an intratextual reading, the connection to other parts of Scripture emerges, which helps us witness to a deeper description of the one we so easily and abstractly describe as friend, redeemer, and savior. But my first point here is to emphasize the importance of *attentive, careful reading*, what I have previously called "lingering in Scripture's room." This is the job of a witness. In sermon preparation we often rush ahead to meaning, interpretation, doctrinal commitments, application, and relevance. The press of the Sunday deadline does us few favors. Thus, we begin by slowing down. With the first question, What do I see? we begin with deferential attentiveness to the text, and we pay attention to when we have inadvertently left Scripture's room.

Reading Scripture as a Single Witness to Jesus Christ

With the second question, Whom do I see? the preacher witnesses to Jesus Christ through the attentive reading of Scripture. The purpose of this second question is twofold: to keep us from leaving Scripture too quickly and to keep our sights on God, in Jesus Christ. As I have listened to sermons and struggled with my own preaching, I have noticed that Jesus too easily falls out of sight. His temptations become

---

1. We could note that the Greek verbs are in the passive voice, indicating Jesus's willingness to allow these events to happen to him. We could contrast Jesus's response to that of his disciple who uses a sword to cut off the ear of a soldier at his arrest. The sword of the Spirit, his Word (Eph. 6), is the only sword Jesus will raise against the powers of evil. Jesus is one whose power is in his Word. Jesus most fully reveals God's nature when he allows the events of Good Friday to happen to him. This student's one observation allows room for a rich description of Jesus's identity.

our temptations; Mary's yes to the angel becomes encouragement to take risks in life. Jesus's incarnation becomes the comforting message, "You are not alone"—and little else. Paying attention to the identity of Jesus keeps our feet in the text. Through the discipline of attentive reading, I hope I am less likely to present an understanding of God unmediated by Scripture. This does not mean that every sermon is about Jesus. It does mean that most of them are.

How do we discern the identity of Jesus Christ as revealed in Scripture? By paying attention to the words and actions on the page, for his identity is given there, not in something hidden or behind the historical Jesus or in intuited motivations or private revelations. God shows himself to us by relating to his unreliable and broken creation—Israel, outcasts, and the church—and by sending his Son in the Spirit to draw creation to himself. The identity of God, revealed in Jesus, is of a God for and with us, and no other. This identity is seen most fully in the death and resurrection of Jesus but is seamlessly joined to what precedes and follows it in Scripture.

Increasingly in the West we are living in a world of constructed identities. In stark contrast to this phenomenon, the theological foundation of these six questions is the claim that the identity of Jesus Christ, revealed in Scripture, is not one of many possible identities. It is not symbolic or arbitrary. It can be no other than that revealed in Scripture, and it is unique to him. Another version of Jesus Christ cannot be substituted for the identity revealed in Scripture. As Auden says, "It could in no way be other than it [was]." This is from "The Meditation of Simeon," and his description of its implications is worth recounting: "By the event of this birth the true significance of all other events is defined, for of every other occasion it can be said that it could have been different, but of this birth it is the case that it could in no way be other than it is. And by the existence of this Child, the proper value of all other existences is given, for of every other creature it can be said that it has extrinsic importance but of this Child it is the case that He is in no sense a symbol."[2] Thus Jesus's identity is, to use the term coined by Hans Frei, "unsubstitutable."[3]

2. Philip Turner introduced me to this wonderful phrase of Auden's. For this and the following quotation see W. H. Auden, *Collected Poems*, ed. Edward Mendelson (New York: Random House, 2007), 388.
3. Frei, *Identity of Jesus Christ*.

This second question, Whom do I see? also springs from the church's conviction that all the Scripture of the Old and New Testaments is a single witness to this unsubstitutable identity of Jesus Christ and is essential to it. To claim that, despite the plurality of human authors, all Scripture forms a single witness to Jesus Christ is to talk about how the Spirit uses Scripture. We will explore this more fully in the next chapter. The Spirit uses all of it, beginning with Moses and the prophets, to bear witness to Jesus Christ in his unity with the Father, who is the God of Israel and creator of the universe.

While it is possible to speak of the unity of the canon in literary terms, here we turn to a distinctively theological unity. All Scripture is providentially ordered by God around the presentation of Jesus Christ. Christ "appears" in all the Scriptures: in creation, in Israel's life and law, in the fate of the nations, in the mission of the church and the end of the ages. In reading and praying all the Scriptures in their entirety and detail, we are conformed to Christ's identity as the resurrected one.

Reading Scripture as a single witness to Jesus Christ has been the norm for most of church history. This is how the disciples read it and how the resurrected Jesus teaches us to read it in order to understand his identity. As described in the previous chapter, this is how the resurrected Jesus taught his disciples to read it on the road to Emmaus and in the upper room (Luke 24:13–35, 44–48). I have often found it sobering that the risen Jesus's in-the-flesh presence among his disciples did not trump the need to study the Scriptures, beginning with Moses and the prophets, in order to know him.

The same declaration is echoed in the story of the rich man and Lazarus. The rich man, now in Hades, pleads with Abraham to send someone from the dead to lead his brothers to repent. Abraham replies, "If they do not listen to Moses and the prophets, neither will they be convinced even if someone rises from the dead" (Luke 16:31). Though as preachers we find inspiration for our sermons among our people; in news, literature, film, or song; in flashes of inspiration; and even in dreams, none of this excuses us from studying Scripture as the risen Christ does with his stunned disciples. Nor are we excused from the need to pray that Christ might open our minds to understand all that is written concerning him. These post-resurrection Scripture studies, along with Abraham's declaration in Luke's Gospel, can boost our confidence that we don't need to wander far afield in order to lay before our congregations the one who addresses and claims them as he does this world and its future. The question that shapes the preacher's practice and vocation is not *where* but *how*. For proclamation, how do we read the diversity of Scripture as a single, complex testimony to Jesus Christ? How do we stick with Scripture—all of it—until we understand how it pertains to Christ and his messianic domination?

The Theological Function of the Narrative of Scripture

The American novelist, essayist, and poet Reynolds Price has written about how he was shaped by Scripture's unyielding pressure on him from the time he was a small child through his difficult adult life, which included spinal cancer and paralysis.[4] Scripture's stories, images, and, most of all, the narrative of the Gospels formed and shaped his imagination, his sense of the world's unity in its creator, and his trust in the singular claim of its pages: *"Your life is willed and watched with care by a god who once lived here."*[5]

Before he was old enough to read, Price's parents bought him a vividly illustrated children's Bible, *Hurlbut's Story of the Bible*, from a traveling salesman. Price is fairly certain that his parents never looked at the illustrations before they gave it to him. He would turn the pages and wonder about what kinds of stories had led to such "swarming" pictures. They were pictures, the kind no longer found in children's Bibles, of scantily clad Old Testament heroines, dripping with anguish and passion. When he learned to read, the Bible's unnerving stories pulled him in. There was Abraham bent on butchering his son Isaac, and David holding the bloody, hacked-off head of monstrous Goliath. Best of all, Price thought, was the glistening child in a strawy stable. When he was a fevered adolescent he turned to the Gospels. There he saw the account of a single life that was tortured and then transfigured by the dark hand of the source of creation. Even as a teen, Price could

4. Reynolds Price, *The Three Gospels* (New York: Scribner, 1996). For the story of his long fight with and recovery from cancer, which includes a vision of Jesus healing him in the Sea of Galilee (on p. 42), see Price's *A Whole New Life* (New York: Scribner, 1995).

5. Price, *Three Gospels*, 13 (emphasis original).

see in the life of Jesus that this hand had not only shaped the actual earth and the lives of its creatures but had also produced, as sparks from their core, the works of his early models and masters—Dante, Michelangelo, Bach, Handel, and Eliot. "My own hopes for my work began to take a big share of the heat from what I thought was the same core—the life of a man who apparently refused to die."[6]

Price often taught courses on the Gospels at Duke University and produced his own translations and introductions to the Gospels of Mark and John.[7] As a writer he had a deep appreciation for the literary structure of Scripture, the mastery of "ideal narrative distance" in Mark and the flights above "the limits of language" in John.[8] Comprehending the structure and strategy of Scripture's narrative gave him deep pleasure and awe. It is, however, Scripture's theological function that pressed down on him from childhood to death. The narrative, its claim on his imagination, Scripture's beauty and light, through which he saw the world and his own work, all led somewhere; the narrative pulsed with a gathering beat toward its consistent revealing of Jesus Christ. Price writes that throughout his years he was able to trust in the promises of the man Jesus of Nazareth, whose identity he first comprehended in John's Gospel. In that astonishing moment, when surrounded by detractors in the temple, Jesus claims to "be one with the sole God of all: Amen amen I tell you before Abraham was, I am."[9]

Price's testimony to Scripture's way with him highlights the often obscured truth that its theological function and literary characteristics are not in some kind of competition for which there is only one winner. To focus on Scripture's theological function in this second question, Whom do I see? by no means asks the preacher to boil the bones and sinews of Scripture's tangled and heated narrative into a clear broth of doctrinal statements. Quite the opposite! This second question, like all the questions in this theological practice of proclamation, calls the preacher to practice over time the skills needed for a disciplined imagination. Reading Scripture theologically is a craft and an art. As with any art form, the artist knows that from the limitations of the medium, beauty arises.

6. Price, *Three Gospels*, 14.
7. These are included in Price, *Three Gospels*.
8. Price, *Three Gospels*, 17, 26.
9. Price, *Three Gospels*, 32.

Price makes two further observations about his coming to trust in Christ, both of which speak to the preacher's vocation to linger in Scripture's room. First, his trust was strengthened by the testimony of the first followers. Scripture was not something to master or leave behind once it yielded its truth. Years of study led to continual marveling at the mysteries communicated there. He says, "I have come to that trust through years of reading and watching the probing efforts of other times and peoples at the comprehension of mystery in their own cultures, through the unimplored early arrival of an uncanny sense of the rightness of one man's claims, but above all from the overwhelming impression of both an emblematic truth and an honest effort at accuracy conveyed to me in the hit-or-miss words and domestic wonders explicitly in Mark's and John's stories."[10]

Second, Price did not need or try to "apply" Scripture to his life, as if it was something outside of his life he needed to bring in. (We will discuss application in chapter 6.) The God he found revealed in Scripture is the spark and source of all. The words on the page, and in his case also the pictures in his Bible, led him to connect the identity of the one revealed there to all of life. This was so not only in his writing but also in the more prosaic work of grading papers, sitting on committees, and struggling with cancer, depression, and paralysis. Price's testimony is good news for the preacher who is worried about making Scripture and the identity of Jesus relevant. This concern is something that often leads us to leave Scripture's room for what we perceive as the more accessible worlds of story and personal example. Price's testimony invites us to pause before we do so.

What do we learn from Price's account of his formation as a person, teacher, and artist by the resurrected Jesus Christ? Price did not read the Bible only or primarily because of its good stories. The narrative has a function not lost on him, even as a child. It reveals the identity of Jesus Christ as the resurrected one—the man who refused to die. And rather than needing to translate this identity into more easily accessible categories, Price could see how this one was the very "heat" of all life, and his own life and work drew its heat from this very one. The narrative reveals God's identity, character, and purposes for all creation and for our lives and work as part of it.

10. Price, *Three Gospels*, 35.

48   Preaching Jesus Christ Today

The Narrative Constitutes the Identity of Jesus Christ

To claim that the narrative of Scripture reveals the identity of Jesus
Christ is to speak of the narrative's theological function or purpose
rather than its literary form. Hans Frei describes this purpose or function as its ascriptive logic. The narrative does not describe, refer to,
or illustrate the identity of Jesus Christ. That would be its descriptive
logic. Rather, it *constitutes* the identity of Jesus of Nazareth and also
of the church. Why? The unsubstitutable identity of Jesus is given in
the particular text of Scripture, through the interaction of purpose and
circumstance in the story, and not "in his inner intention, in a kind of
story behind the story."[11] As Price notes, the Gospels (and most of the
narrative of Scripture) record a chain of acts and a few indispensable
words rather than tell of a single consecutively examined life.[12] While
the identity of Jesus is open to interpretation, it is not of our design or
construction and can be no other than what it is in Scripture.[13]

Tools for Keeping Our Sights on God in Jesus Christ

The practices that accompany this second question focus on Jesus's
identity in relationship with the world around him and with us. Why?
The focus of Scripture is not God's being in and of itself—that is not
the story found in the canon—but God for us and in relationship with
Israel, the church, and all creation. What does Scripture tell, show,
reveal, and describe about Jesus's relationships?

11. By this Frei is claiming that Jesus's identity is only available to us through the
description of his actions, specifically through the display of his obedience in reference
to God the Father and not "by grasping certain of his inherent personal characteristics"
or by seeking the "actual" man apart from the story as a storied figure. See Frei, *Identity
of Jesus Christ*, 102–3, 106.
12. Price, *Three Gospels*, 14.
13. The ascriptive logic of Scripture pointing to Jesus Christ is not limited to its
narrative portions. It is the foundation on which its expository sections are built. The
story of Jesus Christ is presupposed by Paul and the other writers of the New Testament
letters. Paul's letters are an attempt to reflect theologically on the meaning of Christ.
Richard Hays makes the point that Paul's Letter to the Colossians is governed in decisive
ways by Christ's story, even though that story finds only fragmentary expression within
the discourse. Richard B. Hays, *The Faith of Jesus Christ: The Narrative Substructure of
Galatians 3:1–4:11* (Grand Rapids: Eerdmans, 2002), xxiv.

The practices are simple.

1. As you respond to the following prompts, try to make Jesus the subject of your sentences. Describe who Jesus is in the various relationships depicted in the Scripture you are reading. Who is Jesus in the relationship with

   ▸ his Father?

   ▸ the Holy Spirit?

   ▸ his disciples and friends?

   ▸ outcasts or the religious authorities?

   ▸ Israel?

   ▸ creation?

   ▸ the powers of sin?

   ▸ evil and the devil?

   ▸ unbelievers?

   ▸ death?

   ▸ suffering?

   ▸ prayer and the future?

2. What do the actions, responses, or patterns of movement in your text (or in other Scriptures to which your text led you) reveal about the identity of Jesus Christ? Again, try to make Jesus the subject of your sentences.

3. If your text is an Old Testament passage, what might you learn about Jesus that you cannot learn in the New Testament alone? For example, what do you learn about Christ's Passover from the first Passover that you cannot learn from the story of his passion and death alone?

Attending to Scripture's Ascriptive Logic: An Example

Let me offer an example of attending to Scripture's ascriptive logic. In the Revised Common Lectionary, Year B, on the sixth Sunday of Epiphany, the story of Jesus healing the leper (Mark 1:40–45) is paired with Paul's description of himself as an athlete training to win an imperishable prize (1 Cor. 9:24–27) and with 2 Kings 5:1–14 and Psalm 30. In a sermon on these texts, it would be easy to jump into stories of athletes, talk about the favorite sports teams of your congregation, or liken Paul's effort to training for a triathlon. But to do so is to absorb the world of Scripture into today's world of professional and extreme sports and to risk losing focus on the unsubstitutable identity of Jesus. Trying to attend carefully to Scripture's words and sticking with them until they yield the identity of Jesus offers one way to reverse this all-too-easy movement, especially when various demands crowd out time for sermon preparation. Instead of defining Paul as an athlete through the lens of contemporary sports, we should instead do so through the identity of Jesus, whom Paul says he imitates. After doing this we can move to the witness the church bears to the world and to ourselves as we imitate Paul. The homiletical possibilities are many. What might that look like? Here is one possibility.

The Gospel narrative begins as Jesus is proclaiming his message throughout Galilee (Mark 1:39). The leper says, "If you choose, you can make me clean" (v. 40). Jesus so chooses and stretches out his hand. The leprosy leaves the man and Jesus sends him to the priest with the warning to say nothing to anyone. The healed man does no such thing. As we keep reading attentively, we notice that by the end of the story Jesus and the healed man have traded places. Mark writes, "But he [the healed man] went out and began to proclaim it freely, and to spread the word, so that Jesus could no longer go into a town openly, but stayed out in the country" (v. 45). Jesus is now the one who cannot enter the town, and the healed man is now the one who goes around proclaiming freely. This is what Jesus was doing just before he healed the man (v. 39).

This reading might lead the preacher to ask, "What does this narrative detail reveal about the identity of Jesus Christ?" How is his identity shaped by the place he assumes in his incarnation, through the cost of binding himself to humanity, the cost of healing the afflicted, and the place he will take on our behalf in his crucifixion? Reflections on questions such as these, on Jesus's identity, become a frame through which to understand Paul's athletic training and our own as disciples. At a minimum, this interpretation challenges the image of the athlete who pummels her body so she can outrun all her competitors. And that is part of its function. As John Howard Yoder writes, the identity of Jesus as Lord leads us to acknowledge that he is the center that must guide critical value choices. Our sermons are one of the places where we may be called to subordinate or even to reject those values that contradict Jesus.[14] Hopefully this kind of attentive reading will help to prevent the easy absorption of Scripture and the church into the world of meaning and felt needs. One possibility is that the discipline of athletic training, as interpreted through the story of Jesus healing the leper, prepares us not to win races but to come alongside our neighbors and walk with them. It declares to us that to do so is no walk in the park. It takes practice, preparation, and training.

Approaching preaching as a theological practice does not lead to a uniformity of belief or sermon style or form. This approach is compatible with diverse interpretations and practices. It is Scripture's own durability as a fixed text across centuries and cultures that opens the possibility of multiple interpretations. When read attentively and listened to by different generations of preachers captivated by its formative potential in new situations, it bears the fruit of new understandings in new situations.

The Identity of Jesus: An Embrace of Creaturely Differences for a Postmodern World

The beginning of Luke's Gospel describes Jesus's presentation in the temple shortly after his birth (2:21–24). Jesus has been circumcised on the eighth day (v. 21) and now on the fortieth day, in accordance with the law of Moses, the young family comes to the temple in Jerusalem. Mary is purified from childbirth, their firstborn is presented to the Lord, and Mary and Joseph offer the appointed sacrifice of two young pigeons. Many preachers find this passage problematic, since patriarchal structures seem to be encoded within the text. It would be easier to turn away from it, or at least to skip over the details of circumcision and Mary's purification in the temple. But to avoid or flee

14. John Howard Yoder, *The Priestly Kingdom: Social Ethics as Gospel* (Notre Dame, IN: University of Notre Dame Press, 1985), 11.

from its troublesome particularity is to flee from the very means God
has given us in Jesus Christ to love in a postmodern world.

The practices in which Joseph and Mary participate, difficult as they
may be, constitute—perhaps in ways that words cannot—the news and
promise that the angel delivered to Mary and her response. If the unsubstitutable identity of Jesus is given in the particular texts of Scripture
through the interaction of purpose and circumstance in the story, then
the practices of the temple in which Joseph and Mary participate are
deep embodiments of and a kind of outward clarity of Jesus's incarnation and Mary's identity as *theotokos* (God-bearer).[15] Both are rooted in
the reality of creaturely distinction, which Christ embraces—the reality
of creaturely distinctions that are so problematic today.

Rather than flee from these concrete details, we should note how
an attentive reading of them reveals the identity of Jesus Christ as one
who embraces the difficult aspects of being a human today: sexual,
economic, and social. In his presentation in the temple, Jesus *assumes*
rather than negates the sexual and economic distinctions that are part
of being a creature. In response to a postmodern world, which sees
such differences in terms of a struggle for dominance, his incarnation
offers us an alternate way to view, respond to, and inhabit creaturely
differences. We need not choose between negating the chasm between
ourselves and the other or casting it in terms of power. Jesus's identity
offers us a way to love across this chasm.

The scene in the temple in Luke 2:21–24 leads us to the description of these practices in Leviticus 12. In his theological commentary
on Leviticus, Ephraim Radner reflects on the centrality of the twelfth
chapter of Leviticus to the Christian gospel and to the ecclesially based
practice of the work of the preacher.[16] Radner explores the identity of
the church as the body of the *circumcised* Christ. He argues that this
identity is found within the practices of circumcision and ritual purification. In Jesus's circumcision he does not shun the particularities and
limitations of human flesh. His participation in this ritual practice *is*

15. See chap. 5 for a discussion of the inner and outward clarity of Scripture.
16. Radner, *Leviticus*, 9–14. This series is based on the conviction that dogma clarifies
rather than obscures the interpretation of Scripture. It advances the assumption that
the Nicene tradition, not as a formula but as a habit of mind, is the proper context for
interpreting Scripture.

his identity as one who embraces and redeems creaturely differences and inequalities.[17]

Radner tackles the implications of blood, semen, male, female, clean, and unclean as marks of our nature as creatures limited and marred by the inescapable reality of time and history. Blood, Radner observes, is tied up with the reality of a people who exist in time and whose relationship with God exists in time. Blood is given for the continuance of life (childbirth), blood is taken for the ending of life (Cain), and blood is shed for its redemption (Jesus).[18]

Leviticus 12:6–8 describes the ritual practices prescribed for women at the end of their ritual purification. Two sets of instructions are given; their difference is based on the economic status of the family of the woman who has given birth.

> When the days of her purification are completed, whether for a son or for a daughter, she shall bring to the priest at the entrance of the tent of meeting a lamb in its first year for a burnt offering, and a pigeon or a turtledove for a sin offering. He shall offer it before the LORD, and make atonement on her behalf; then she shall be clean from her flow of blood. This is the law for her who bears a child, male or female. If she cannot afford a sheep, she shall take two turtledoves or two pigeons, one for a burnt offering and the other for a sin offering; and the priest shall make atonement on her behalf, and she shall be clean.

Mary and Joseph cannot afford to buy a sheep for a sin offering. Mary's offering of two turtledoves or young pigeons (as prescribed by the ritual practices) instead of a lamb (Lev. 12:8; Luke 2:24) establishes Jesus as a creature taking his place in a world of creaturely differences and material poverty. In God's selection of Mary and Joseph, God sends his Son into a world of material inequality. In circumcision, Jesus fully takes up this world of distinctions and temporality. He is born of a

17. Radner, *Leviticus*, 120–34.
18. Radner wonders if the uncleanness associated with childbirth—whose exact nature is explained nowhere in Scripture—has to do with the ambivalence of blood's historical character. "Blood contains in its passage into and through the world the whole history of freedom, choice, sin, oppression, forgiveness, suffering, sin's outcome, and some kind of redemption through it. The woman's childbirth is all of this at once and hence gives rise to and embodies the fullness of history" (*Leviticus*, 125).

woman whose blood embodies the world Jesus will not shun. He is born into a family of material poverty. His participation in circumcision, with the shedding of his own blood there, renders his identity because "it functions as an explication of who Jesus is and the nature of his body as one who is in the world: Jesus assumes distinction, he does not abolish it."[19]

Where does such attentiveness to a scriptural description of Jesus as one who assumes sexual, economic, and other inequalities as part of being created in time lead us? Given the historical reality of these practices, what is our vocation as Christian preachers who take our place within a community of hearers in and for a world of distinctions and divisions? The text presents enormous challenges to our self-understanding and ecclesial vocation; in doing so, it offers us a possible way forward in our vocation to love God and neighbor. We do not need to leave the world of creaturely differences for the more sanitized world of principles, ideals, or abstract truths. Attentiveness to the text also allows us to preach such love, refusing to flee its location. Our attentiveness to love is located *within* the chasm of creaturely givenness and incommensurability, anchored there in Christ's own embrace of this strange world. Love does not negate or erase creaturely differences. "It is the nature of love that it be exposed to and embrace this incommensurability of otherness."[20]

The Preacher as Witness to Christ

In the first of the Six Questions, What do I see? the preacher begins sermon preparation as a witness to what she sees in the fixed text of Scripture. Attentiveness to Scripture is both a spiritual practice and, as described in the introduction, a divine remedy for the temptation to look away from what offends. Here, with the second question, Whom do I see? the preacher moves into the more focused practice of seeing Jesus Christ in Scripture's storied world.

Paul Ricoeur's description of the particular nature of biblical testimony is helpful in highlighting the preacher's role as witness to

19. Radner, *Leviticus*, 122.
20. Radner, *Leviticus*, 122.

Christ. Biblical testimony does not belong to the witness. This is what distinguishes the biblical use of testimony from its uses in ordinary language. "It proceeds from an absolute initiative as to its origin and its content. It comes from somewhere else and is about the global meaning of human experience, which is Yahweh himself."[21] Ricoeur's description echoes the claim that the function of Scripture is to reveal the identity of Jesus Christ. This is the vocation and privilege of the preacher: to testify to God in the narrated events in Scripture—not to testify to other things, to point to ourselves and our experiences and struggles, or to abstract truths or universal experiences.

Knowing that the identity of Christ is revealed in the narrated events of Scripture is enormously helpful to the preacher. It directs our attentive gaze and locates it with the creaturely distinctions of the strange and wondrous texts of Scripture. Preaching is a burden, and often the preacher longs to lay down the weight of having something to say week after week. In the midst of this routine the enormous privilege of what we are called to do can get lost. Through the years of our ministry, we immerse ourselves in Scripture and train our eyes to see there what is promised: "The Word became flesh and lived among us, and we have seen his glory, the glory as of a father's only son, full of grace and truth" (John 1:14). To direct our gaze to see in Scripture's pages the one every eye will see (Rev. 1:7), such is the privilege of sermon preparation. This is the one before whom we will stand at the last and see as our friend and not a stranger (Job 19:25–27).

---

21. Ricoeur, "Hermeneutics of Testimony," 131.

3

"What Is Christ's Word to Me?"

The Preacher as Confessor

▶ **Main action:** Hear God's address to you and receive God's mercy and judgment.

In a series of meditations on the daily nature of faith, Kathleen Norris begins with some information about the American poet Sylvia Plath.[1] Toward the end of her life, Plath decided to stop washing her hair. She did so because she knew she would only have to wash it again. And again. Plath could no longer abide the daily nature of much of living, having to wake up and do it all again. Parents of young children know this. Those who live with a chronic illness or a disability know this. So do preachers.

Preachers wake up Monday morning knowing they have six days to turn it around. Six days to get ready for the following Sunday. During those six days, they prepare for and participate in the scheduled

1. Kathleen Norris, *The Quotidian Mysteries: Laundry, Liturgy and "Women's Work"* (Mahwah, NJ: Paulist Press, 1998).

57

activities of the week: Bible studies, meetings with community leaders, hospital visits, midweek prayer services, and pastoral conversations. They carve out space to plan for future events like the ecumenical food pantry, the Bible study in the local café, the Christmas services, and next summer's mission trip. They also respond to whatever contingencies or emergencies arise: the arrest of a parishioner, a funeral, a flood in the church, a natural disaster. Did any clergy have 9/11, Hurricane Irma, or the massive wildfire in Fort McMurray, Alberta, penciled in their calendars? Of course not.

You get it done and then the following Monday you wake up and do it again. And again. It is not the rhythm of school or the university with semesters, exam week, spring break, and summer vacation. When students ask if they can turn a paper in late, I remind them that there are no extensions on Sunday morning. It is not the rhythm of the office or corporation, where months can be devoted to a single project, account, or client. It is not even the rhythm of the farm with its seasons, harvests, and fallow times. The rhythm of the dairy farm is close. Every morning you wake up and the cows are still there.

Somewhere in our three dimensions, preachers need time and space to attentively read the Scripture for the following Sunday and crank out another sermon. If you are lucky, you might not have to preach every week. Most of my students serve small or multipoint parishes in the vast landscape of Canada. Recent graduates tell me that what they were the most unprepared for is the demand of preaching every week.

The Hazards of Preaching

The hazard in all this is that the sermon becomes one more thing to get done before Sunday morning, and Scripture becomes one more thing in our week we need to manage—so we can come up with the final product, the sermon, and get to bed. Reading Scripture as part of sermon preparation becomes one more thing to be accomplished in a week already filled with too many demands. This is the hazard of preaching: Scripture becomes an object to study (often quickly) or a diving-off point for our own reflections on what we think the parish needs or wants to hear. When pressed, we latch on to an easily available meaning, tell some stories, and make do. Or we dust off an old sermon or download something from the internet and make a few changes. Then we wake up Monday morning and have six days in which to do it all again.

What gets lost in this is our knowledge of what Scripture is and what it does. For all practical purposes it becomes a text that is primarily in our hands, not in the Spirit's, a text with which we must figure out something to do, rather than a text that does something to us. The living, active Word of God becomes something we deal with rather than letting it deal with us. Our roles as witness, confessor, and theologian get shelved for the more expedient role of—what? Reading Scripture for preaching as a spiritual discipline gets shelved until we find some breathing room in our week or a way to go on retreat. The cost is high for everyone.

Questions 3 and 4 of sermon preparation (What is Christ's word to me? and, What is Christ's word to us?) are a reminder to try not to let this happen. They are a reminder that the parish—clergy and congregation together—is a community of hearers of God's Word. They are based on the knowledge that how we approach and read Scripture for sermon preparation makes a difference. These two questions weave into the weekly practice of sermon preparation the spiritual discipline of putting ourselves in a position to be addressed by the text and, through God's Word, to listen for Christ's word to our congregation. They try to create space for this twofold movement, which is a particular spiritual discipline of preachers. Through our congregations, God continues to form us into his sons and daughters. The gift of growing into the full stature of Christ over time is not just for ourselves but for those to whom we are joined and whom we serve. The preacher Thomas Breidenthal described the double movement of the spiritual practice of those who preach and pastor. This is the moral practice that lies at the heart of preaching, "placing oneself as preacher in a position to be addressed, probed, and dissected by a scriptural text, *so that through one's own preaching on it*, the text can intrude upon God's people with grace and power."[2]

How can we put ourselves in a position to let the text in the Spirit's hands take hold of us? Do something to us? Awaken us? Speak a word

---

2. Breidenthal, "Sharper Than a Two-Edged Sword," 41 (emphasis mine).

to us? And through us and our sermons speak a word to our congregation? How do we help them listen with us to the Word? To pose these
kinds of questions about sermon preparation is to approach this weekly
task as a spiritual practice.

To speak of weaving into our practice of sermon preparation questions that invite us to approach this weekly task as a spiritual discipline
can sound a bit like killing two birds with one stone. Or trying to get
kids to eat vegetables they dislike by hiding them in the meatloaf. Questions 3 and 4 are based neither on expediency nor on multitasking but
on an understanding of what kind of text Scripture is in the Spirit's
hands and how God prepares us to receive it. Scripture addresses us
across cultures and centuries, and God gives us the ears to hear this
address, likewise across cultures and centuries. These theological commitments about the nature of Scripture are the foundation of any understanding of preaching as a spiritual practice. They are the foundation
of questions 3 and 4. They also are solid ground for the difficult tasks
of reading and listening to the fixed text of Scripture and then daring
to preach it across the divides of our postmodern world. It is God who
speaks and it is God who gives us the ears to hear. This is good news
for postmodern preachers.

The Holy Spirit Creates Hearers of God's Word

In his lectures on Genesis, Luther works out this foundational aspect
of the divine-human relationship. The Word is God's essential and
constitutive element in his relationship with the world. God's Word
addresses us, and this same Word creates our ability to hear it. Jaroslav Pelikan, in his introduction to Luther's sermons on the Gospel of
John, writes, "Luther contended that whatever God might be in and
of Himself apart from the created world, in the creation He had put
relations between Himself and the world upon the foundations of the
Word of God."[3] Luther writes,

> God does not speak grammatical words; He speaks true and existent
> realities. Accordingly, that which among us has the sound of a word is

3. Luther, *Luther's Works*, 22:51.

a reality with God. Thus, sun, moon, heaven, earth, Peter, Paul, I, you, etc.—we are all words of God, in only one single syllable or letter by comparison with the entire creation. We too speak, but according to the rules of language; that is, we assign names to objects that have already been created. But the divine rule of language is different, namely, when He says: "Sun, shine," the sun is there at once and shines. Thus the words of God are realities, not bare words. . . . He created the world and all things with the greatest of ease, namely, by speaking. There is no more effort for God in His creation than there is for us in the mention of it.[4]

This fundamental aspect of the divine-human relationship is seen in creation, in God's relationship to Israel, and in Jesus Christ. Jesus is both the proclaimer of the Word and the Word itself. At the beginning of the Gospels, Jesus's arrival is marked by his proclamation of the Word: "The kingdom of God is at hand" (Mark 1:15 ESV). Charles Campbell points out that the Word of God, the sword of the Spirit, is the only sword Jesus will raise against the powers of this violent world (Eph. 6:17).[5] Jesus takes up this divine sword—the Word spoken and in the flesh—both in his proclamation and as he is lifted high on the cross. As Karl Barth says, "The word of God is the act of God. . . . There is no point in looking about for a related act."[6]

Both Ezekiel's preaching to the dry bones of the house of Israel and Jesus's raising of Lazarus testify to God's ability to make us hearers of the Word. In both stories the ability to hear God does not come through any anthropological, political, physical, or existential claim. The Lord commands Ezekiel to preach to the dry bones of Israel. "Prophesy to these bones, and say to them: O dry bones, hear the word of the LORD" (37:4). Ezekiel does so, and through his preaching the house of Israel hears God's promise: "I am going to open your graves, and bring you up from your graves, O my people; and I will bring you back to the land of Israel" (v. 12). In John's Gospel Jesus stands before another set of dry bones, the corpse of Lazarus. Here Jesus speaks directly to the dead man: "Lazarus, come out" (11:43).

4. *Luther's Works*, 1:21–22.
5. Charles Campbell, *The Word before the Powers: An Ethic of Preaching* (Louisville: Westminster John Knox, 2002), 48.
6. Karl Barth, *Church Dogmatics* I/1, ed. G. W. Bromiley and T. F. Torrance (New York: T&T Clark, 2009), 143.

An obvious point in this pair of stories is that bones have no ears and dead men cannot hear. Only God can make the bones of Israel and the corpse of Lazarus able to hear God speak. The witness of Scripture is that God has done just this. In Luther's lectures on Genesis, he writes, "As the private Word spoken into the unformed mass of heaven and earth creates life out of nothing, so too God's public Word as Gospel spoken into the hearts of humans creates faith in them."[7] In his sermon on the opening of John's prologue Luther writes, "In the end only the Holy Spirit from above can create listeners."[8]

In God's constitutive relationship with the world, God has created us with a common identity despite our differences and divisions. You and I, whether we live in Haiti, Halifax, or Helsinki, are all Lazarus's and Israel's dry bones. We are listeners created from above, regardless of whether we are immigrant or native born, straight, gay, liberal, conservative, minority or majority world, vegan, or a member of the National Rifle Association. We might seem oceans apart from our neighbor in so many ways and on so many issues, but despite our differences, in terms of this fundamental posture before God, we are all in the same boat. We are all dry bones who have been addressed by Jesus Christ. All peoples, races, nations, generations, and cultures stand together on the same side of the divide between God's Word and our ability to hear it. The gulf is there, but too often we mislocate it and in doing so miscalculate the distance between ourselves and others. All or any of us—no matter how wide our differences—are only able to hear God's Word because in that same Word God has opened our ears (Ps. 40:6). God in Jesus Christ has crossed this divide and given us all ears to hear him. As the psalmist says, "This is the LORD's doing; it is marvelous in our eyes" (Ps. 118:23). And this is good news to preachers. Because of the promise that God has given us all ears to hear him—because of this hope and no other—preachers dare to proclaim the Word of God to their diverse congregations and to claim their vocation to help all persons listen together to God's address.

7. John Headley, *Luther's View of Church History* (New Haven: Yale University Press, 1963), 19.
8. Luther, *Luther's Works*, 22:8.

Sermon Preparation as a Spiritual Practice: Submission to the Word

Sermon preparation as a spiritual discipline or practice takes its shape from Christ's sacrificial love. As described in the last chapter, Christ's incarnation and presentation in the temple reveal his embrace of creaturely differences. His identity offers us a way to love across this chasm. The posture we take before the Word in sermon preparation is shaped by this love, which has embraced and redeemed creaturely differences. Christ's embrace offers us a way to listen across the chasms between ourselves, our congregation and cultures, and the often strange text of Scripture. That way is Christ's subjection and sacrificial love. It is the stance of Christ's self-giving life and humility, which the church describes in its creeds and enacts in its sacraments and practices.

Can we, as have Augustine and many others, learn to listen to Scripture in order to preach to our diverse congregations? To listen with an ear for how Scripture speaks not just to us but to the whole church? We share this challenge and privilege. How do we preach today to the wide variety of persons God has entrusted to us, with their various backgrounds and depth of Christian knowledge? How do we preach to those who are suspicious of Scripture, those who do not know its basic story, those who have gone to Bible college, or those who have been practicing Christians most of their lives? How do we preach to such a wide range of needs, situations, and starting places? With Augustine, we do so by putting ourselves in a position to be addressed by the Word and, moving through this essential spiritual practice, to hearing it not as a word only to one person in the privacy of their study but as a word to their diverse congregation.

We read all Scripture by the rule of mutual corporate submission. This is the shape of Jesus's own sacrifice of love. This practice emphasizes our stance in front of the text: humility, not suspicion. It asks us to allow the text to be the subject that addresses and works on us, rather than an object we stand outside of to analyze. A practice of humility or mutual submission means we do not close our eyes or ears to any text (or to any neighbor).

We hold lightly our certainty of what a text means. For example, to skim over or dismiss Ephesians 5 because it speaks of wives being subject to their husbands is to close our ears to its deeper call. By sticking with it, we can hear its call to both husbands and wives to practice mutual submission to one another in Christ. There the call to be subject to one another is not an expression of creaturely inequality but a demonstration of the love formed by Christ, who stands in the midst of our limitations and there gives us power to love as he does. We are called to submit to one another out of reverence for Christ (5:21). But we fail to learn from Christ and to be in Christ when we justify our inability to love someone different from us—whose difference challenges us—because of the gap between us.

Usually our suspicion of or discomfort with a text is a sign to read more deeply and widely, using the tools given for the first question, What do I see? In *On Christian Teaching*, Augustine chastises would-be preachers over their too easy dismissal of difficult texts: "If anything appears there which seems absurd, you, like all foolish people, do not find fault with yourself . . . , but rather find fault with those books which, perhaps, are simply unintelligible to minds such as yours."[9] In the article "Teaching the Bible Confessionally in the Church," Ellen Davis describes the need to read Scripture with openness to repentance.[10] She notes that one of the important features of the multivoiced character of Scripture is that it exposes our tendency to read it in order to maintain our own self-interests. Reading with an openness to repentance is a guard against too easily identifying ourselves with Jesus (what would Jesus do?) and conflating his sinless life with ours.[11]

Putting ourselves in a position to be addressed by the text is an ill-defined spiritual discipline because it encompasses so much. What goes into it? Everything. Our study, our exegetical work, our knowledge of Greek and Hebrew, our theology, our intratextual reading, our knowledge of the people in our congregations, our evangelical zeal. Our own repentance, and the times we have received God's mercy and grace. The hours at the desk or in the library or chapel. Our heart. Our ego. Yes, all these and more. Like all spiritual disciplines, the purpose of this one for sermon preparation is to till the soil—and no more. That is, the purpose is to make us more able to receive God's Word, grace, judgment, and mercy. This spiritual practice, like all others, does not manufacture or

9. Quoted in Kolbet, *Augustine and the Cure of Souls*, 123.
10. Ellen F. Davis, "Teaching the Bible Confessionally in the Church," in Davis and Hays, *Art of Reading Scripture*, 16–18.
11. Davis, "Teaching the Bible," 16–17.

create love and knowledge of God, but it can create the conditions in which we come to recognize and receive God's gracious gifts. The promise of all spiritual disciplines is that in the tilled soil God will indeed plant his Word. For preachers this means, in part, that a sermon is on its way.

Dietrich Bonhoeffer also impresses this discipline on would-be preachers. The preacher does not ask what a text has to say to other people. The preacher does not ask how he is going to preach or teach this text; rather, the preacher asks what it is saying directly to him.[12]

> In our meditation we ponder the chosen text on the strength of the promise that it has something utterly personal to say to us for this day and for our Christian life, that it is not only God's Word for the Church, but also God's Word for us individually. We expose ourselves to the specific word until it addresses us personally. And when we do this, we are doing no more than the simplest, untutored Christian does every day; we read God's Word as God's Word for us.[13]

The claim that sermon preparation is a spiritual discipline is based on this hope: that the Holy Spirit uses this weekly task for God's ongoing formation of his tired preachers, and through them the people they are bound to in the church. In this mortal life, God's truth and transforming power are held *only* in transient wrappers—the difficult words of Scripture, our feeble sermons, our broken people, our flawed church. But in the incarnation, Christ has made these creaturely limitations his own. God has made these broken vessels our road to the end to which they point, Jesus Christ. It is here—and nowhere else—that we find our vocation as preachers and pastors: to live within the fleshly limitations of the human condition and the strange words of Scripture with hope and expectation, knowing that Christ has redeemed both.

Practice for Question 3: What Is Christ's Word to Me?

What does Christ say to me through the Scripture I am listening to? Here we build on the attentive work done in the first two questions.

12. Dietrich Bonhoeffer, *Life Together: The Classic Exploration of Christian Community* (New York: Harper & Row, 1954), 82.
13. Bonhoeffer, *Life Together*, 82.

What has caught our eye in the movement of a passage, a line of Paul's argument, an oracle from a prophet, a detail in the narrative, or a connection to other texts? Through the lens of what and whom we have seen, in questions 1 and 2 we listen to what Christ says to us. While our answers need not be breakthroughs (though they could be), we must listen to his Word echoing across the terrain of our own lives. We do not skip this step.

Here are some questions or tools to facilitate our hearing. Our responses to the third question should be about us—our lives, world, and ministry: Christ is saying to me . . . I hear him saying . . .

- Am I hearing something that offends me? Scares me? Makes me angry or sad?
- Am I hearing something that Christ has been trying to tell me in Scripture that I don't want to see or hear?
- Am I hearing something I need to hear about his Word? His world? My fears, my purpose, my family, my vocation? The church?
- Am I hearing his response to my faithlessness, my insecurity, my wounds, my jealousy of others, my pride?
- Am I hearing something about how God wants me to love? To repent? To ask for forgiveness? To speak boldly?
- Am I hearing God's mercy? God's judgment?

An Example

Let me try to put myself in a position to be addressed by the one who calls forth a response from us and who is God's response to our sin. Here I continue with the passage of the rich man (Mark 10:17–27), which I looked at in chapter 1. Through an intratextual reading of that story I was led to other stories: the wedding guest without a garment, Jesus before Pilate, and the suffering servant. My ears latch on to verses 21 and 22: "Jesus, looking at him, loved him and said, 'You lack one thing; go, sell what you own, and give the money to the poor, and you will have treasure in heaven; then come, follow me.' When he heard this, he was shocked and went away grieving, for he had many possessions."

As I listen, I notice that the rich man seems to assume he has to do the hard work of giving up his possessions and following Jesus on his own. Which, of course, he cannot do. Is this why he does not ask Jesus for help, for mercy, for power to do the very thing he has asked of Jesus? Why is he unwilling to say, "I don't think I can do this on my own. Jesus, please help me do what you've asked of me"? His unwillingness or inability to ask for help becomes more glaring in light of Christ's explanation of this encounter to his disciples: "Jesus looked at them and said, 'For mortals it is impossible, but not with God; for God all things are possible'" (v. 27). Jesus did not, it seems, expect that the rich man could do it on his own. Or that anyone else could.

The question of why the man didn't ask for help becomes the place where Christ addresses me through the text. As I allow myself to be probed by God's two-edged sword of grace and judgment, I am led to acknowledge my own ambivalence about standing before Jesus. I worry that I will be unwilling to give up my comfortable life if he asks that of me. In moving beyond the specific exchange between Jesus and the rich man, I acknowledge how hard it is for me to ask for help even in ordinary situations. Through the rich man's silence when faced with his limitations, God speaks to me of my response to my limitations. Rather than leading me to ask for help, they lead me to shame and silence. Even when I am standing in front of Jesus.

This causes a long-forgotten memory to resurface. I remember canoeing down the east branch of the Penobscot River in Maine when I was a young graduate student, unwisely trying to navigate class 5 rapids. The canoe overturned. I was swept down the whitewater river, bumping from one rock to another. Though I was in no position to get out of the river by myself, I didn't cry out for help, even after I managed to grab onto a rock. As I was swept downriver, out of the corner of my eye I saw another graduate student pounding down the path along the river, trying to catch up with me. He did, jumped onto the rocks, reached down, caught my bruised arm, and dragged me out. "Why didn't you yell?" he asked me.

By putting myself in a position to let God address me through the story of the young man's silence, I am led to explore and confess my own silence before God. This silence is often born of shame and fear in the face of my own limitations. Putting myself in a position to be addressed by Christ leads to a confession of the connection between my silence and my shame and fear.

A practice and posture of humility and mutual submission can counter our resistance to Scripture's witness to God's steady love and judgment. Breidenthal writes, "If I keep my resistance steadily in mind, and bend over backwards to counteract it, it is just possible that the text will manage to get the upper hand, and, like a partner leading me in a dance, will set the agenda for the conversation."[14] The text has led me from the story of the rich man to a story of my own life. But I am not done. There is grace to come.

The Move from Preacher as Witness to Confessor

With question 3, What is Christ's word to me? the preacher moves from the role of witness to confessor. She will move into the role of theologian of the body shortly, but this third question is a necessary practice on the way. We can only make a confession about something we have witnessed. Our role as a theologian of the body is of little use to our congregation if it does not spring from our own confession. The Six Questions form a hermeneutical circle, as do the preacher's roles of witness, confessor, and theologian.

In her role as witness, the preacher first must subject herself to the Spirit's work with the text. She must engage the text and, more so, let it engage her. This is the posture of preachers: to stand under the two-edged sword of the text and allow it to read them and their assumptions and agendas, even as they try to impose these on the text. But this is not what a preacher preaches—her experience of being read by the text and the stories that accompany it. Her sermon is born in her hearing of the text, but she does not preach her experience of hearing it. This distinction marks the move from confessor to theologian and highlights the unique location of the preacher within the community of faith as both disciple of and servant of the Word.

Because we do not preach primarily our experience of subjecting ourselves to the Word's work on us, it is tempting to skim over or altogether skip this third question and the practice that arises from it. The preacher must resist this shortcut because this posture marks a faithful

14. Breidenthal, "Sharper Than a Two-Edged Sword," 35–36.

witness, which is the preacher and pastor's vocation. Ricoeur describes this openness to allowing the text to engage us as characteristic of true and faithful witness: "The engagement of the witness in testimony is the fixed point around which the range of meaning pivots. It is this engagement that marks the difference between the false witness and the faithful and true witness."[15] The engagement of the preacher in her own testimony means that in preaching she *cannot stand outside of it*. She must risk allowing herself to be addressed by the one of whom she has testified, Jesus Christ. This engagement aptly describes the position of the preacher within the interpretive community: she is both the one who *testifies* and the one who, along with her people, *hears the testimony*. She is not narrating what she has seen only for others to hear. She is part of the congregation, the interpretive community. Thus she puts herself in a position to let Christ address her.

Each preacher's spiritual terrain has different ridges and valleys, wastelands and springs. It is a hard thing to let Christ address us in the contours of our spiritual landscape. Wounds, blind spots, vanity, and pride are exposed and dissected. But his address is also a point of relief because Christ's word to us is a word that can be preached as well. When the text judges me, "I know a sermon is on its way and it's going to be all right."[16] The spiritual discipline of letting the text address us will get us to where we need to go, which is Sunday morning, with a sermon in our hands or on our tablet. At this point a sermon is on its way, but there is more preparation to come. The remaining questions help the preacher to shift the focus from her experience with the text to the common journey of faith.

---

15. Ricoeur, "Hermeneutics of Testimony," 130.
16. Breidenthal, "Sharper Than a Two-Edged Sword," 40.

4

QUESTION 4

"What Is Christ's Word to Us?"

The Preacher as Theologian

▶ **Main action:** Hear God's address to the church and one's own congregation in its particular context.

In my former parish in southern Colorado, a group of parishioners were working to reopen a 1,100-acre church camp in the untouched foothills of the Sangre de Cristo Mountains. This effort involved both renovating the aging facilities to bring them up to the current building code and creating a business plan to make the camp financially viable. Without that, the land would most likely be sold to developers. Two parishioners, men in their late forties, were heavily involved in this project. The first parishioner lived in his van in the church parking lot. His alcoholism had cost him his job, his family, and his home. The second was a surgeon in one of the local hospitals. They both loved the mountains and shared a vision of what the camp could become: financially self-sufficient and ecologically responsible. On Sunday afternoons, they would drive up to the camp in the first parishioner's van.

There they walked its dirt roads with a map and a set of blueprints in their hands for ten 100-acre "green" home sites.

If it were not for the church, the only place these two men were likely to cross paths was at the surgery table. Yet each Sunday, together they listened to the Word of God, prayed, sang, confessed their sins, received Holy Communion, and joined in the fellowship and mission of the church. Both learned to listen together to the Word within the body of Christ across the wide chasm of their social and economic differences. One from the pews, the other from the choir stalls.

The Movement from Question 3 to Question 4

If we liken the Six Questions to a road the preacher travels in sermon preparation, we come to a bend in that road as the preacher moves from question 3, What does Christ say to me? to question 4, What does Christ say to us? With question 4 the preacher turns from her own experience of hearing the Word for herself to hearing it as Christ's address to the church. She does not ignore it or cast it aside as a personal word. Rather, holding it loosely, she keeps listening to the appointed Scripture until she has discerned something of what the Spirit is saying to her congregation as part of the one church with one mission across time. This is a turn from the subject to the church. It is a turn from receiving God's word primarily through one's own perceptions and felt needs to trying to listen to it corporately in the church.[1] It is the movement from witness and confessor to theologian.

This turn from the subject to the church is based on the knowledge that our own experiences and personal narratives are too small a stage

1. The modern turn to the subject takes concepts involving the subjective self (such as the idea of the individual, autonomy, autonomous reason, self-consciousness, and subjectivism) as the foundational categories for human flourishing. The philosopher Charles Taylor provides an influential (and optimistic) exploration of Western culture's evolution from what he calls an "enchanted society" where humans are at the center of a universe designed by God to "exclusive humanism" in which belief in God is both optional and problematic. Charles Taylor, *A Secular Age* (Cambridge: Harvard University Press, 2007). See also Charles Taylor, *Sources of the Self: The Making of Modern Identity* (Cambridge: Cambridge University Press, 1992). For an accessible introduction to the writings of Charles Taylor see James K. A. Smith, *How (Not) to Be Secular: Reading Charles Taylor* (Grand Rapids: Eerdmans, 2014).

for hearing and preaching the Word of God. Chapter 6 addresses in detail the uses and limits of personal experience and story. Suffice it to say here, our small lives and needs, whether our own or those of our parishioners, are simply not a large enough stage on which to hear and understand God's address. Pulpits are meant for more. There we testify to and confess Jesus Christ, the Son of the God of Israel, who acts in the contingencies of our lives, our congregations, the nations, and the world as part of salvation history. Salvation history, given in the full sweep of Scripture, lived out in the history of peoples and nations and embodied in the church through the ages, is the only stage large enough for interpreting our own experience of hearing God.

Question 4 is also based on the theological conviction that the double movement of the Holy Spirit is corporate. The dual function of the biblical narratives is to create a people with an identity disclosed to them in the narrative and to form them as people capable of hearing that story. The Word is given to the people of God—to Israel and the church. Through the Spirit's use of it, God creates a people with an identity disclosed to them in the Word and *also* forms them into a people capable of hearing that Word. Question 4 calls preachers to locate their role as clergy *within* the identity the Word offers to all people, clergy and parishioners alike, as hearers of the Word. Preachers try to close the gap between clergy and congregation, not by dismissing differences but by taking our place among our people as hearers of the Word in the interpretive community of the church.

The double movement of the Spirit locates us in at least three "communities" of people formed by Scripture to be hearers of the Word. First, preacher and people are part of the story of Scripture itself. The fixed texts of Scripture, the canon, were put together for the future communities of this church. The early church, the church of the book of Acts, is the same continuous church to which we belong. Second, preacher and people are part of a local congregation, the local "interpretative community" with its own narrative and cultural, denominational, and historical shape. Finally, preacher and people are part of the future of this single continuous community, which one day will gather around the heavenly throne. As we will see later in the chapter, the Magnificat, or Mary's song (Luke 1:46–55), models the movement involved in turning from placing ourselves in a position to be addressed personally by

God's Word, to listening with and on behalf of our congregation as part of the one church with one mission across time. Mary preaches and sings on the wide stage of salvation history. She is a witness, confessor, and theologian to God's address.

Question 4 locates the preacher within and among the people of her congregation. Starting with our shared identity as hearers of God's Word does not negate the importance of the various social locations of the preacher and people in hearing, interpreting, preaching, and enacting Scripture. It does not dismiss the gap between clergy and people. It does not dismiss or devalue the need to educate one's congregation in the task of preaching.[2] Finally, it most certainly does not negate the need to work for equality and justice. What it asks for is a critical assessment of the ordering of these multiple contexts—our shared identity as hearers and our multiple social contexts. Question 4 seeks to order them epistemologically. The psalmist says, "Hear this, all you peoples; give ear, all inhabitants of the world," and only then goes on to describe the peoples' social contexts: "Both low and high, rich and poor together" (Ps. 49:1–2). This is our hope and God's promise.

Closing the Gap: Our Shared Identity as Hearers of the Word

Rooting a practice of preaching in the shared identity God offers through his constitutive relationship with the world helps to close the gap between clergy and people. The shape and size of that gap differs from denomination to denomination. As an Anglican minister, I wear a clerical collar and robes during worship, which sets me apart visually from my congregation. But I am in a network of accountability to my bishop, the parish council, and the *Book of Common Prayer*, which limits my individual power. Some of my colleagues in Baptist or independent churches wear dresses, skirts, shirts, and jackets while leading worship and thus visually appear no different from the members of their congregations. Because my colleagues work in independent churches with less structured ecclesial authority and worship liturgies, they have far more personal power than I do in my vestments. Whether emphasizing

2. See Tisdale, *Preaching as Local Theology and Folk Art*.

the priesthood of all believers or the authority of the magisterium, no single denomination has a corner on misusing the power and privilege of ordination. Lifting up the shared identity of preacher and people as those God has given ears to hear him is not to imply that this is easily within reach. The misuse, abuse, and neglect of the preacher's and of the congregation's authority is common. The church that receives its life and form from Jesus Christ, as Richard Hooker reminds us, is an assembly of "the sound and sick alike."[3]

Thus question 4 is based on a communal hermeneutic: we listen, interpret, and respond together. The focus of Scripture's interpretation for preaching shifts from text and interpreter to Scripture and community.[4] Understanding the congregation as an interpretive community, of which the preacher is a part, situates preaching within the web of practices of the church. Preaching is not the only practice through which people learn to listen to and interpret Scripture within its ecclesial and social locations. Situating the preacher within this web of practices further locates the authority of the preacher in the task of equipping all, including herself, to hear Christ's address to the church.

Augustine's life and work demonstrate the purpose of question 4. He understands his vocation as inviting inquirers to become a part of the Christian community and teaching them to become hearers of the Word. His vocation as priest, bishop, pastor, and preacher is set in his larger vocation as one to whom God had given ears to hear, and in his acknowledgment that the church was a school for developing the single skill needed to listen and love. In a sermon on James 1:19–22 (thought to have been preached in his hometown of Thagaste), Augustine confesses this primary and shared identity: "My brothers and sisters . . . I tell you that what gives me really solid satisfaction is listening. I repeat,

3. W. Speed Hill and Georges Edelen, eds., *Of the Laws of Ecclesiastical Polity: Book V*, vol. 2 of *The Folger Library Edition of the Works of Richard Hooker* (Cambridge, MA: Harvard University Press, 1977), 68.15.

4. Stanley Fish first coined the phrase "interpretive community" in *Is There a Text in This Class? The Authority of Interpretive Communities* (Cambridge, MA: Harvard University Press, 1980). Charles Campbell argues that Hans Frei changed his hermeneutical position from a general literary approach (based on the genre of realistic narrative) to a particular "communal hermeneutic," which focused on the church's tradition of literal reading. His key categories become not text and interpreter but Scripture and community. This is akin to Augustine's means of interpreting Scripture. See Campbell, *Preaching Jesus*.

the time my satisfaction, my joy, is really solid and unalloyed is when I am listening, not when I'm preaching."[5] His goal is not to pass on the biblical text's authority merely for reception but to create a community where all are hearers of God's address. He is confident that the inquirer's perceptions will be shaped by the ongoing task of listening to Christ speak in the Scriptures, as Augustine's own have been.

Augustine tells those who come to hear him that despite the fact that he is the one preaching, "We are all hearers."[6] He follows this with sentiments including, "join in with me"; "help me knock at the door"; "I am your fellow worker"; and "let us both listen together, both learn together."[7] He sees the task of preaching as helping the congregation learn to listen to Scripture speaking. Paul Kolbet, in *Augustine and the Cure of Souls*, writes of Augustine, "His task was not to expound his own opinion but to interpret the scriptures. . . . [He gives] the text itself a voice." Kolbet quotes Augustine, who says, "Listen to holy scripture preaching. . . . It is Christ who is doing the teaching. . . . His school is on Earth, and his school is his own body. The head is teaching his members, the tongue talking to his feet."[8]

Listening and Learning Together

Augustine claims this vocation for himself, along with his people. "You cannot despise the remedy offered to others and not yourself."[9] Augustine likens himself to a hired hand who cultivates trees from the outside but lacks all ability to make them grow or produce fruit. He is not the physician of their souls; he is looking to be cured along with them.[10] He begins Homily 32 by providing his hearers with instructions on how to participate in the homily; he invites readers to join him in a shared inquiry into the meaning of the Scripture, which leads to self-knowledge and personal transformation. He structures his homily around inquiry into specific biblical texts. "I am prompted by the Lord to tackle together with you this text that has been read and

---

5. Augustine, *Essential Sermons*, ed. Daniel E. Doyle (Hyde Park, NY: New City, 2007), 236.
6. Kolbet, *Augustine and the Cure of Souls*, 165.
7. Kolbet, *Augustine and the Cure of Souls*, 184–85.
8. Kolbet, *Augustine and the Cure of Souls*, 176.
9. Kolbet, *Augustine and the Cure of Souls*, 160.
10. Kolbet, *Augustine and the Cure of Souls*, 177.

find out what it means. If you have seen the question, you have seen no small thing."[11]

The preacher engages in the task of helping her congregation learn to listen attentively with her to Scripture. This shared listening can mitigate both the preacher's exclusive authority to hear and interpret the Word and the passivity some parishioners feel toward engaging Scripture themselves. However, an understanding of a shared identity as listeners can be misused to exclude those who challenge or upset that shared identity. If this happens, the congregation needs to keep listening—to Scripture and one another—together.

Our Two Contexts

The fourth question, What is Christ's word to us? is a reminder to the preacher that she must listen and pay attention to two crucial contexts.[12] The Spirit's work is textually mediated both within the particular contexts of the believer—her social, racial, political, and economic contexts—*and* within the context of belief. Let me explain. I read Scripture as a Christian, that is, as a person who holds beliefs and commitments about God, the world, Scripture, the church, and so on. So do my colleagues on Baffin Island in the Arctic. None of us read it as disinterested persons—that is, objectively. We read it, one in Inuktitut and the other in English, because of what we hold to be true about the world. We read it with and from within our congregations and churches where it is read, preached, and enacted in worship, mission, prayer, outreach, and discipleship. This is the context of belief. We also both read Scripture within our different social, economic, and geographic contexts. Thus how Scripture speaks to us—that is, how we receive God's Word to and about us (questions 3 through 5), will vary despite our shared context of belief. Both contexts are essential and cannot be disentangled.

While traffic between the two contexts runs both ways, the preacher must decide their relationship to one another. We will always listen to Scripture through our embodied selves. How can we do otherwise? But

11. Kolbet, *Augustine and the Cure of Souls*, 184.
12. See Yeago, "Bible: The Spirit, the Church and the Scriptures." I am indebted to his description of the two contexts for much of what follows in this section of the chapter.

we must also resist the tendency to stop there, to listen solely through this lens. Our creation as listeners to God's Word is the soil in which all our socially conditioned identities take root. The context of belief is what sets the interpreter, the text, and the culturally specific situation in relationship with one another and brings them to bear on one another. In other words, we learn how to interpret our various social locations and divisions through Christ's embrace of creaturely differences, not the other way around. We do not begin with an understanding of our social contexts derived independently from Scripture. We turn to what Scripture teaches us about such differences through its own texts. This is the hermeneutical approach of question 4.

We can do so because of the fixed text of Scripture. Though historically and culturally specific, Scripture's narrative itself—and nothing else—lets us know that the God rendered in Scripture, and not another, is at work outside of Scripture's immediate referents. Scripture describes the entire created world because there is only one world and it is God's—all of it, including all the smaller created worlds that compose our reality: families, nations, cultures, the future, the past, and on and on. Because of this, Scripture is able to describe all worlds, even our worlds beyond its immediate referents, claiming that they are one in God's sovereign ordering. The tree of life in John's revelation is for the healing of the nations, understood in their fullness. Thus Scripture defines what it means to be fully human and how human beings take their socially and economically rooted place within God's creation. Scripture also defines what it means to fall short of the gift of our humanity. As Yoder has said, we know more fully from Jesus and in the context of the confessed faith than we know in any other way.[13]

Learning from Christ: The Embrace of Inequality as Divine Action

Christ's incarnation is God's embrace of human distinction and division in the most sweeping way. Christ leaves behind all equality with God and, desiring to be born in human likeness, takes on the form of a slave (Phil. 2:5–7). Could any form more fully inhabit human division, differing social contexts, and inequality than that of a slave? Christ is

13. Yoder, *Priestly Kingdom*, 11.

born while Palestine is under Roman occupation. He is born to poor parents who participate in the cleansing rituals appointed by Torah, rituals that draw distinctions between women and men, poor and rich. Young boys are slaughtered by Herod after Christ's birth because of their sex and age. Jesus begins his life as a refugee in Egypt, not unlike the millions of recent refugees from Syria who fled first to Egypt and Turkey and then throughout the Mediterranean, Western Europe, and Canada. These social, sexual, and economic distinctions are the inevitable reality of creaturely existence in a fallen world. Christ does not shun them. He does not exist in a world of abstractions, nor does he capitulate to using these distinctions for his own gain. He embraces and redeems them, and in so doing gives us the light through which to gaze on and respond to the inequalities of creaturely realities. That light is his redemptive love of creaturely existence. "In [his] light we see light," the psalmist says (36:9). This is the divine epistemology we try to bring along as we listen to Scripture with our congregations. Can we develop the skills to learn to interpret and respond to creaturely divisions as part of apprehending the incarnate wisdom expressed in Christ and his embrace of such divisions? Such is our vocation and privilege with and among our people for the sake of Christ and the world.

There is no neat distinction between one's social location and the context of belief. As noted earlier, traffic moves both ways. Our beliefs shape the kind of significance we give to social locations and our own self-interests and vice versa. Try spending time reading the Bible with refugees in order to understand the crucial need for both contexts. To say refugees read the Bible only to find out what it says about their political and economic status as strangers, who most often are poor, is to yield to the postmodern temptation to reduce the interpretation of texts to a series of moves in a struggle for dominance. Christian refugees read the Bible to do more than figure out which parts are in their own interest. They read the Bible not only because they are poor and refugees but also because they are people of faith and part of the community of God. They read the Bible because of what they hold to be true about God, themselves, the world, poverty, the biblical texts, and God's future. In it they hear Christ address them in their situation. This is because Scripture reveals the identity of the one who is Lord of all the nations and "who executes justice for the oppressed; who gives food to the hungry" (Ps. 146:7). Likewise for those who are not poor or refugees. For persons of faith, for whom welcoming the stranger and lifting up the downtrodden is urgent, it does not complicate hermeneutic technique to interpret Scripture as addressing them as well.

What Is Christ's Word to Us? Hearing the Word as Divine Continuum

This guideline for hearing Scripture as a word to the church comes from the claim, as described in chapter 2, that the textually fixed discourse of Scripture is the single address of the Spirit to the church across time and contexts. It is always a word to us within this larger context. Question 4 emphasizes the continuum of divine purposes. It asks us to keep listening until we have discerned something of what the Spirit is saying to our own congregation as part of the one church with one mission across time.

While this kind of listening might not be well practiced, it is good news for the tired preacher. We don't have to erect the bridge between Scripture and its meaning for our congregation. We don't have to figure out how these strange old words correlate with the current concerns of our people. Instead, we must be willing to be theologians in a way appropriate for the pulpit. Rather than "use" Scripture as a resource to speak meaningfully to the horizon of needs and desires of a particular congregation, we interpret it as God's corporate address that *prescribes* for us the horizons we ought to live within.[14] This corporate address, within the continuum of divine purpose and divine action, establishes the stage on which the drama of our lives takes place.

Relevance is not established by coordinating the text with the expectations, perceptions, and felt needs of the hearers, but by bringing the hearers themselves into the realm (inhabited alike by Paul, the Corinthian believers, and the contemporary church) where the intentions articulated in the text hold sway.[15]

Liturgy establishes the context in which the church gathers and knows the purposes of God. Liturgies of all kinds begin with an invocation of the Holy Spirit and a proclamation of Christ's death and

---

14. Yoder, *Priestly Kingdom*, 87–88.
15. Yoder, *Priestly Kingdom*, 88.

resurrection. As we gather, we declare who we are and how we live: as a people formed in the context of Easter and Pentecost. We are the body of the risen and ascended Christ, commissioned to bear witness to him in the world.

Stanley Saunders and Charles Campbell point to the central place of liturgy in the preaching of the Word. In "Anything but Ordinary" they argue that defining the long liturgical season of ordinary time (which runs from the Monday after Pentecost until the first Sunday of Advent) by the Christian narrative of eschatological time compels us to ask, "What is ordinary for Christians?" Worship, they write, provides the answer.

> When we worship, it is not important that, for example, we are bankers, or teachers, or housewives, that we are males or females, or that we are poor, rich, or middle class. Nor does it matter what part of the world we come from, or what color our skin is. During worship we enter into space where the phones (usually!) do not ring, where there is no television or radio, and where the assumptions and relationships that govern our lives in the business world or at the shopping mall or in the home do not prevail. Rather what does define us during our worship—and this alone—is our common relationship to the God of Jesus Christ.[16]

Worship, they argue, "redescribes the world," not solely through its social structures and our fractured and contested identities but through the new reality we share in Jesus Christ.[17] All stand together in need of God's life-giving Word. We stand as those whom God has not abandoned; in grace, God has given us ears to hear him. This shared identity does not erase distinctions, as discussed above, but situates the vocation of the preacher within this shared identity.

Mary as Model for Listening to Scripture in a Postmodern World

In Luke's telling of the nativity story, the angel addresses Mary specially and directly. How could she not listen? But focusing primarily on Mary's social context, her youth, her economic and marital

16. Stanley P. Saunders and Charles Campbell, "Anything but Ordinary: Worship and Preaching in Ordinary Time," *Journal for Preachers* 18, no. 4 (Pentecost 1995): 28.
17. Saunders and Campbell, "Anything but Ordinary," 30.

status, or even her obedient assent to the angel's message misses the
wider context of belief in which Mary's hearing is rooted. The wider
context is God's promises to Israel and the practices of the temple,
and it becomes the stage on which Mary sings her sermon. Though
Scripture tells little about Mary's personal faith, it is worth noting
that Mary and Joseph knew, despite her youth, the practices of the
temple (prescribed in Lev. 12) and participated in them. Thus, we
can cautiously surmise that Mary had a wider context for hearing
the angel's very personal and strange message, and that context is
a context of belief rooted in the textually mediated story of salvation
and the practices of the temple.

Her song indicates three ways she "heard" God's address. Mary
heard it personally, within God's larger purposes for Israel and within
her economic and social context. Though Gabriel's message was a
personal address, and she responded to it as such, God's promises to
Israel are the soil in which this personal address is heard and rooted.
Mary interpreted and proclaimed the personal address in the context
of God's larger actions. The favor shown to a lowly handmaiden, the
honoring of her name throughout the generations, and the good
things God has done for her do not stand alone. They are part of the
larger narrative of God's remembering and fulfilling his promises to
help Abraham, Sarah, and their descendants by helping Israel. Within
this context of belief, here belief in God's promises to Israel, Mary
names lifting the poor and casting down the rich, filling the hungry
and sending the rich away empty (Luke 1:52–53). In her proclamation, the Magnificat, Mary responds to the angel's message; she is
witness, confessor, and theologian. She has attentively listened to
Gabriel and heard his message as a word to herself. But she keeps
listening, keeps pondering the message in her heart, until she hears
it as part of the single Word given to God's people in the continuum
of God's promises.

Tools for Interpreting God's Address

This list of questions is to be used in the theological interpretation of
God's address to you for your congregation:

- What is God saying to us, through what I heard him say to me in Scripture, about his Son?
- What is God saying to us about the life we share in his Son?
- What is God saying to us, through my experience of being touched by God's Word, about how he is using the church to accomplish his purposes today?
- What is God saying to us about the vocation of our congregation in this time and place?
- How does this word speak of the shape of our lives as Christians?

What Is Christ's Word to Us? An Example

Here is an example of moving from question 3 (What does Christ say to me?) to question 4 (What does Christ say to us?). I pick up with an earlier example, where we aimed to put ourselves in a position to be addressed by God's Word. For the purpose of exemplifying the move from question 3 to question 4, we will dissect a single movement into small, painstaking steps. What follows is akin to learning to move through the gears on a manual transmission. Very quickly it becomes a single, fluid movement. The text is the story of the rich man (Mark 10:17–26). As described earlier, I listen to Christ's address to me in that text and respond with a specific question: Why didn't the rich man ask Jesus for help? After the rich man asks, "What must I do to inherit eternal life?" Jesus responds, "You know the commandments. . . . You lack one thing. . . . Sell what you own. . . . Then come, follow me" (vv. 19, 21). Mark writes that when the man heard this, he went away grieving, for he had many possessions (v. 22). The silence of the rich man led me to confess my own silence before God and to acknowledge that my silence often is born out of shame and fear. It evoked an old memory of my inability to cry out for help as I was swept down a river after a canoeing mishap.

The movement to question 4, What does Christ say to us? is difficult. I could tell the story of my own silence as I was swept downstream. The image of my fellow paddler pounding down the path in an effort to try to catch me would make an appealing Christ image. I am fairly certain, however, that my congregation would remember the story rather than any connection I made to Scripture or to the risen and ascended Christ. I resist the temptation to include it in my sermon. Though I do not use the story in my sermon, I do not fully discard it in sermon preparation. It is the doorway through which I try to enter into the Spirit's word to the congregation—but only a doorway. I need to keep listening until I can hear this Scripture as a corporate address within the continuum of divine purpose and divine action.

My point of entry into this text is the rich man's silence in the face of Jesus's response. As I turn the corner to hearing this as a corporate address and helping the congregation listen together, I pay attention to the two contexts of my congregants: their social contexts and the context of faith. Does it matter to hearing this as a corporate word that the man is rich? Does it matter that his possessions are his undoing? What about my parishioners who are poor, who have left everything behind to immigrate to Canada? How will they hear it? What about the members of the congregation who are rich? By the world's standard I am rich. Can I hear it as a word to all? These reflections then lead to a larger question I pose to myself: Can my own point of entry into hearing this as a word to me—the rich man's silence, his inability to ask Jesus for help in letting go of his possessions—be a point of entry for the community of interpretation whose members have different economic locations? I hope so, but I come up with no clear answer.

Next, I try to view the rich man's economic context through the context of faith. As said above, we learn more about our various social locations and divisions through Christ's embrace of creaturely differences than in any other way. In his response to the rich man, Jesus shows us the context for understanding our material possessions. We understand them from *within* community, whether it is the community of the church or the larger society we are part of.[18] This reality is here laid out in Jesus's command to the rich man to sell his possessions, give to the poor, and then follow Jesus. In this command Jesus proclaims that we cannot understand the purpose of material possessions in isolation from others, that is, when we see them as belonging only to ourselves and existing only for our own uses. His invitation to sell them and give

18. Turner makes this point in *Christian Ethics and the Church*: "What I 'own' is indeed mine, but its meaning remains hidden until what I 'own' becomes for me and for others the means by which I participate in and contribute to the larger life of society" (204).

the money to the poor (with whom we are in community) is an invitation to the rich man and to all who listen to see their possessions through this light. It is an invitation into a new reality, the one proclaimed as we gather and announce Christ's death and resurrection—the one the rich man is invited to follow, as are we.

Only here, as we stand before God among others (and see all we have and all we are through and for the building of this stance) can we be perfect, to use a scriptural description. After keeping most of God's commands (Mark 10:20), the young man still lacks this posture. He can only see his possessions as belonging to himself. He leaves silent, sorrowful, and alone, "for he had many possessions" (v. 22). Our possessions, as well as our various gifts and abilities, are given to us as means for creating bonds between ourselves and others, the "we" in which each of us is found in Christ.

Here is the beginning of a corporate word and the beginning of a sermon. To preach only this, however, would be to preach Jesus only as the one who makes this invitation, and not to preach Jesus as the fulfillment or "antitype" of our failed responses. In his silence on the cross Jesus becomes our silence, whether for shame, fear, uncertainty, or sin's suffocating weight. The church announces the new reality that we are not left alone in our silence. Unlike the rich man, we can respond to Jesus, saying, "Help me do what I cannot do." Like the blind beggar we shout out in repentance to the one who waits to receive our prayers.

Question 4: What Is Christ's Word to Us?

The preacher's experience of letting the text read her is the place her sermon is born. In her sermon she does not tell the sermon's birth narrative; she does not tell stories of her experience with the text, the memories and confessions elicited and the grace offered. Breidenthal describes the difficult movement from testifier (and confessor) to theologian:

> I have been confronted and healed by the word, and I owe it to myself to return again and again to that experience in prayer. But as far as the sermon goes, my encounter with the word is of no use unless I can shift the focus from me to the Christian journey as such. The preacher

is not first and foremost a testifier but a theologian, and theological reflection is nothing other than the self-subordinating generalization of our religious experience so that everyone can see his or her own walk with Christ reflected there.[19]

The preacher is not left on her own to figure out what this corporate address or collective encounter might look like. The common journey of faith within the continuum of divine promises is described in the church's central teachings about discipleship, witness, creation, mission, sin, vocation, the Triune God, and so on. The content and shape of the church's teachings are found in its liturgies, creeds, mission, sacraments, and confessions—all of which, as said above, are the primary form of the interpretation of Scripture.

Augustine insisted that God's remedies in Scripture were most effective when given voice in the context of Christian liturgy.[20] Scripture and preaching, baptism and Eucharist, are all means by which the Holy Spirit captivates the minds of preacher and people together. Over time the Spirit works to help us see that Scripture and sacraments share a single purpose in the Spirit's hands: to point the gathered people to the singular love of God from which both derive their reality. Texts can become wine, sacraments can be visible words, taken up again and again as an ongoing training in perception, which shapes action as it reawakens and reorders love.

---

19. Breidenthal, "Sharper Than a Two-Edged Sword," 41.
20. Kolbet, *Augustine and the Cure of Souls*, 163.

5

"What Is Christ's Word about Us?"

The Preacher as Theologian of a Broken Body

▶ **Main action:** Describe the identity of the church and the disciple
given in Christ's word and address to us.

We Are What He Has Made Us: A Shared Identity
That Is Not Coercive

I was leading a two-day seminar on baptism and discipleship for new
clergy in the diocese of Toronto in the Anglican Church of Canada.
It was part of a two-year post-ordination training program. The first
day we looked at New Testament passages referring to baptism, the
corresponding sections of the baptismal liturgy in the *Book of Alternative Services*, and the emphasis in each on our participation in Christ's
death and resurrection in baptism. We discussed the promises made
in baptism, discussed preparing adults and children for baptism, and
worked through many case studies. The new clergy were engaged,
vocal, and grateful.

The next morning we turned to discipleship. Together we worked up a list of what a new Christian needs and deserves to know about the Christian life. What can I expect to feel? How will my worldview change, my relationship with my family, my friends, the environment, issues of justice? What if I'm not sure I made the right decision? And so on.[1] Though the group came up with a thoughtful list of questions the church needs to explore with the newly baptized, the clergy were restrained and disengaged. I could tell something was off. When I asked them about the lukewarm participation, their answer surprised me. It was the word "disciple." They found it problematic, especially across theological lines. The clergy who had grown up in conservative churches said it reminded them of their restrictive childhoods. "I was told that I couldn't wear shorts," one young man said, "because I was a disciple of Jesus Christ." Some who identified themselves as liberal felt it did not leave enough room for one's personal journey with Christ. "I used to be a therapist," another participant said, "and it doesn't seem right to tell people what it means to follow Christ." Happily, or so it seemed at first, everyone preferred the word "formation" to discipleship. Until one participant got out her Bible and read Jesus's command at the end of Matthew's Gospel: "Go therefore and make disciples of all nations, baptizing them in the name of the Father and of the Son and of the Holy Spirit, and teaching them to obey everything that I have commanded you" (28:19–20).

What does it mean for our preaching if a group of new clergy, who span theological lines, who have bound themselves to God's Word and God's people in the church, resist straightforward biblical terms for our shared identity in Christ? Their pushback raises this question: How, if at all, can we speak of a shared identity in Jesus Christ in ways that do not seem coercive? Or exclusive? Or empty? Is this shared identity merely deposited at the doors of the church when parishioners leave?

If we do nothing or leave it to each parishioner to sort out who they are in Christ, we fail to proclaim Scripture and the power of God's Word at work in those to whom God has given the ears to receive it. "We are what he has made us," Paul writes (Eph. 2:10). At the most

---

1. We worked from an essay by William Abraham: "On Making Disciples of the Lord Jesus Christ," in *Marks of the Body of Christ*, ed. Carl E. Braaten and Robert W. Jenson (Grand Rapids: Eerdmans, 1999), 150–66.

fundamental we are creatures because we are made; we are creatures whose mortality, because Christ has taken on our deaths, has become a vessel of divine grace. We are also his body, the church, which is God's act, not ours. "God made Eve of the ribbe of Adam. And his Church he frameth out of the verie flesh, the verie wounded and bleedinge side of the Sonne of man."[2] Question 5, What is Christ's word about us? is a question about what the Word does or creates in us. And to what end? To ask what Scripture does is to ask a theological question.

With question 5 we move on from attentiveness to the text (What do I see?), from the identity of Christ revealed there (Whom do I see?), and from his personal and corporate address to us (What is Christ's word to me? To us?). Here in question 5, we turn to discerning the identity he gives us through his word—that is, to discerning the body. Hooker describes this as a mystical union: "For in him wee actuallie are by our actuall incorporation into that societie which hath him for theire head and doth make together with him one bodie" (cf. Col. 2:9–10; 1 Cor. 12:12).[3] By virtue of this mystical conjunction, we are of him and in him, just as if our very flesh and bones were an extension of his (Eph. 5:30). The movement of the first five questions, from sight to hearing to recognition, is theologically driven by the double movement of the Holy Spirit. The resurrected and ascended Christ, who is revealed in the text, speaks to us and creates in his word a people with an identity in God's mission to the nations.

The difficulty of discerning and proclaiming—and then living out a shared, corporate identity—is no small thing. We are all called to personal faith in Jesus Christ. Jesus asks each of us, as he did Peter and the others, "But who do you say that I am?" (Matt. 16:15). We are called to confess him as Christ, the Son of the living God, to follow him, and to be his witnesses in the world. At the same time we are called, as Paul says, to discern the body of Christ as we gather (1 Cor. 11:27–29). We share a unity with one another in Christ, which, like our identity as hearers of God's Word, is God's creation, not ours. This unity is hidden in Christ (Col. 3:3) and is only found in him, not in abstract principles, right teaching alone, or a universal humanity

2. Hill and Edelen, *Laws of Ecclesiastical Polity: Book V*, 56.7.
3. Hill and Edelen, *Laws of Ecclesiastical Polity: Book V*, 56.7.

(Eph. 2:11–22). The identity God gives us in Christ, as Martin Luther King Jr. learned at Ebenezer Baptist, is "a community that is joined by race, family, neighborhood, and economics, but whose truest identity transcends all of these."[4]

The combination of Protestant piety, with its emphasis on a personal relationship with God, and Western culture, where the self is recognized, prioritized, and indulged, makes an understanding of the shared identity God has given us in the body of Christ an uphill battle at best. We lament what the lone wolf of individualism has done to a sense of community in the West, and yet we fiercely guard the right to individual self-definition and autonomy from oppressive communal restraints.

Throughout Scripture the corporate identity of Israel and the church is named through wide-ranging descriptions, titles, and images. They are not given as pieces of information or a kind of report. In the Spirit's hands these identities claim us and call forth a response. God names Israel "called" (Isa. 48:12), "my son, my firstborn" (Exod. 4:22; Jer. 31:9), and "my servant" (Isa. 41:8; 44:21; 49:3). Israel is to be a holy people (Deut. 7:6–8), a chosen people (Deut. 7:6; Ps. 135:4; Isa. 41:8), and a light to the nations (Isa. 49:6) but is also compared to a silly dove (Hos. 7:11). Israel is a green olive tree (Ps. 52:8; Jer. 11:16) and, in its disobedience, an oak whose leaves wither and a garden without water (Isa. 1:30). Likewise the church is the body of Christ (Eph. 2:22; 4:15–16), a vineyard or a vine (Mark 12:1–12; John 15:1–8), a building "not built by human hands" (2 Cor. 5:1 NIV), the bride of Christ (Mark 2:18–20; John 3:29), God's handiwork (Eph. 2:10 NIV), and God's field or garden (1 Cor. 3:9). This list is not meant to be either exhaustive or systematic but to reveal Scripture's broad description of the identity God has given to Israel and the church. These names are a reminder that it is God who has made us and God who names us.

Can we, as preachers and pastors in our various contexts, discern the body and recognize and participate in the unity God has given us in Christ? Can we proclaim that identity, as Scripture does, without it being heard as an oppressive communal restraint or in fact becoming so? It is harder than we would like to believe.[5] It is our vocation.

4. Lischer, *Preacher King*, 79.
5. David Lose argues that the preacher needs to create the necessary safety and distance for people to appropriate the gospel for themselves. See *Confessing Jesus Christ*, 55.

Sermons are meant to build the church. The fifth question of the sermon, What is Christ's word about us? asks us to consider the place of the church in God's mission and in our preaching.

This might seem like a bad time for anyone to put all their eggs in a particular ecclesial basket. The church's misuse and abuse of practices and peoples, its divisions, decline, and tepid witness in the West are all reasons for which its practices are suspect. "Spiritual but not religious" is a code phrase for people who look outside the church for the Spirit's handiwork. In one of my classes we discuss just this. In a recent class we read the first few chapters of Paul's Letter to the Ephesians. We came to Paul's description of the place of the church in God's plan for the fullness of time: "That the manifold wisdom of God might now be made known through the church to the rulers and the authorities in the heavenly places" (Eph. 3:10). I asked the students, who came from an array of denominations, how they thought the universal church was doing on this score. There was silence, marked by heavy hearts. After a bit, one student asked, "Is there a plan B?" Not as far as we know. We do know, however, that the Holy Spirit both creates *and* judges the church (1 Pet. 4:17).

The Spirit, the Church, and the Scriptures

The Six Questions of the Sermon are based on trying to interpret Scripture for preaching in a way that is consistent with how we understand the Spirit to use it. Throughout this book I locate the inspired character of Scripture in the Spirit's use of it, not in its writing per se or in matters of form. To say the biblical texts are inspired is to say that the Spirit has formed and made these texts to advance God's ongoing mission. Here with question 5, What is Christ's word about us? I turn to the relationship between the Spirit, Scripture, and the church, and to questions of the church's corporate identity. An attempt to pin down how the Spirit uses Scripture and the church in God's mission could be misconstrued as a nail in the coffin of the Spirit's freedom. To speak of the key role of the church in the interpretation of Scripture could also be misconstrued as implying that the church creates Scripture and that there is no distance between the text and what the church makes of it. The Six Questions of the Sermon are not a formula or method for preaching Spirit-filled sermons, despite what we might wish. I hope that by trying to suggest how the Spirit uses Scripture and the church, the preacher might have a better idea of what to do with both in preaching. At best we can put ourselves in a position to encounter the freedom and authority of the Holy Spirit through God's gift of Scripture.

The Spirit uses Scripture to form, build, judge, and correct the church as its witness to the nations. The relationship between Scripture, the church, and God's mission in the Spirit's hands is summed up in the fine phrase of David Yeago. His phrase is clear, accessible, and teachable: "The Spirit bears witness, and *the church is the witness the Spirit bears.* . . . Scripture is the standing testimony of the Spirit to the church, for the purpose of forming the church itself as the Spirit's testimony to the nations."[6]

It is the Spirit's work to build the church as the public witness to Jesus as the Son of the God of Israel, and to the God of Israel as the Father of Jesus. The Spirit uses Scripture to do just this. The Spirit uses Scripture to address the church. Through the same Spirit, the church listens; its response of a common and public life of practices, repentance, and mission is the Spirit's witness to the nations of the resurrected Christ.

Two points need to be emphasized. First, the Spirit's mission is to make visible to the nations the power and wisdom of God that is present in the crucified Messiah. The public and visible nature of the church is essential. Whatever words we use in sermons to articulate our discernment of the body—our corporate identity—the fact remains that the visible and public character of our shared identity is not optional. Second, the Spirit's work is always textually mediated in Scripture *and* in the life of a people. The earthly, historical community of the church, the renewed Israel gathered to the crucified and risen Messiah, *is* the sign that the Spirit plants on earth as its witness to the Father and the Son. I will take these two points in order.

---

6. Yeago, "Bible: The Spirit, the Church and the Scriptures," 63 (emphasis original). Yeago's understanding of Scripture's inspired character has influenced the development of this chapter. He presents a doctrine of inspiration that is renewed in two ways. First, his goal is to retrieve earlier notions of the inspiration of Scripture without retreating into a doctrine of plenary inspiration or of premodern exegesis. Second, he refuses to locate the Spirit's work primarily in formal matters of canon and language studies. He locates it in the use the Spirit makes of Scripture.

To What End? The Spirit's Mission

One of my favorite images from John's revelation is a description of the nations in his vision of the New Jerusalem in chapter 21. This city has no temple, sun, or moon because God is its light. Through its pearl gates the kings of the earth will bring their glory and the people will bring the glory and honor of the nations (Rev. 21:24–25). I imagine this parade of nations as a kind of divine "show and tell." Other than stating that nothing unclean, false, or abominable will be brought in (v. 27), we are left to imagine what the people and kings carry in their arms as they stream to God's throne. Penicillin? The dismantling of apartheid in South Africa? Chinese fireworks? The 2016 Chicago Cubs? Whatever they carry, the point is that the nations are streaming to God's throne on which sits the Lamb. Here is the end to which the Spirit's work is directed. It is the nations' recognition, reception, and worship of Jesus Christ, Lord of the nations. It is their recognition, reception, and worship of him as the resurrected one, who through his death and resurrection raises the dead and makes things new. Their parade around his throne, carrying their best and brightest, witnesses to that power.

The life of Israel and the life of the church are bound up together in the Spirit's mission. The sending of Jesus, the one the nations acknowledge around the throne, is "that [God] might create in himself one new humanity in place of the two" (Eph. 2:15). Jew and Greek, far off and near, friend and stranger: the unity of the two—that is, joint membership in the household of God, is God's work in Christ, and it witnesses to the unity of God. Paul describes it as the mystery of God's will and "plan for the fullness of time" (1:9–10). God's plan is "to gather up all things in [Jesus Christ], things in heaven and things on earth" (1:10). This is a sobering description of God's work and is a judgment of our times, when any common identity is, at best, met with suspicion. Yet this is who God has made us. By incorporating us into the body of his Son, God has overcome the greatest division of all and has made us one with him. "I in them and you in me, that they may become completely one, so that the world may know that you have sent me and have loved them even as you have loved me" (John 17:23). The body of Christ, the church, is the form of divine unity.

Describing the church as the Spirit's witness to the nations speaks of the essential character of the church as public and visible. Placing the church in the center of the hearing and interpretation of Scripture, through worship and practices of enactment, leads to understanding it as more than a theater or public gathering place for a group of disparate individuals to hear a sermon or participate in worship. The church is the locus of the Spirit's work, with a distinctive place in the Spirit's mission as public witness to the resurrected one. Thus, it is appropriate to talk, as some have, of a "pneumatological ecclesiology."[7]

The Distinctive Place of the Church and Its Practices in the Spirit's Work

A few years ago I was attending my childhood church in Washington, DC, on the Sunday after Christmas. I expected the congregation to be thinner than usual, given the day. But I discovered a happy crowd, many people in their thirties. An infant was baptized. Were the kids just home for Christmas and doing the baptism to make the grandparents happy? Or was this a family bringing their child forward for baptism as an expression of their own faith? As a visitor I couldn't tell.

It is difficult not to observe a church service with a professional eye when you are in the business yourself. It was all straightforward, which is a plus in my book: singable hymns, well-read Scripture, a solid sermon. Until we got to the baptism. The *Book of Common Prayer* baptismal service is beautiful and, most importantly, is shaped by and saturated in Scripture. The young priest (the rector had the Sunday off) kept adding bits, annotating it you might say, as if on its own it wasn't enough. He added an informal prayer to ask the Holy Spirit to come down (hadn't we already done that?). He asked a special blessing on the child, that the Spirit might lead the child to truly know Jesus as Lord

---

7. Reinhard Hütter argues that Luther, in his description of the church's core practices in *On the Councils and the Church*, opens the way for a "pneumatological ecclesiology" and suggests that "the church is to be understood as a web of core practices which at the same time mark and constitute the church. These practices are the Spirit's works through which the Holy Spirit enacts his sanctifying mission in the triune economy of salvation." See Hütter, *Suffering Divine Things: Theology as Church Practice* (Grand Rapids: Eerdmans, 2000), 35; cf. *On the Councils and the Church* (1539), in Luther, *Luther's Works*, 41:143–78.

when she was older. Ah, here was my clue! I don't think he believed that the real action of the Holy Spirit happened in baptism (especially of an infant). And he was doing all he could within the context of the liturgy to make up for it.

In the Anglican Church, with its emphasis on set forms of worship, it is easy to be skeptical of the Spirit's action in prayers written long ago. A colleague in a church in Toronto keeps apologizing for the prayers and explains them to the congregation (many of whom are lifelong Anglicans) before they are given the chance to actually pray them. In any denomination the question of where one looks to find the action of the Holy Spirit is a good one to ask in that it unveils what for most of us is unconscious.

At Wycliffe, we expect MDiv students of all denominations to participate in morning or evening prayer when they are on campus. Some tell me they do it only as an act of obedience. The real place they feel the Spirit working in their lives is not in corporate worship but as they read Scripture alone in their rooms. One student was taught she had to read five chapters every morning. Quantity was important. Others, perhaps like the young priest at the baptism, might think the real action of the Spirit is outside the forms of the church—in the inner working of a believer's heart and his personal acceptance of Christ as savior, perhaps in a personal testimony over coffee at Starbucks. For others, it's the opposite. The older the prayers, the better. A non-Anglican Wycliffe student who was going to Trinity Seminary in Singapore in a seminary exchange program asked me if he could borrow a prayer book from the chapel to take with him. I handed him the 1983 *Book of Alternative Services*, which is an updated version of the *Book of Common Prayer* in Canada. "No," he replied, "I want the 1928 one."

There is no easy or single answer to this question of where one looks to find the real action of the Holy Spirit, and competing answers are a reason churches split and new denominations form. Listen to the conversations around infant baptism in the refectory and classrooms at Wycliffe and you'll get the point. It is an important conversation to have. We pay more attention to the places where we think the Holy Spirit is at work and skip over things we regard as hokey, tiresome, or simply external forms. It shows up in our preaching as well. The recognition of our blind spots is part of the call to humility. Paul reminds

us that we are to build up and never tear down (2 Cor. 10:8; 13:10). A
visiting preacher in my former parish once criticized the naïveté of the
motto What Would Jesus Do? (WWJD), which in the 1990s showed up
on T-shirts, coffee mugs, bumper stickers, and bracelets. The middle
and high school Sunday school classes were in the congregation that
morning, listening to this sermon. They were teens from a variety
of backgrounds and families, across economic lines—whose gangly
wrists were all encircled by their own brightly colored WWJD bracelets.

The Spirit's work of making visible the power and wisdom of God
present in the crucified Messiah is always textually mediated in Scripture and in the life of a people. Many would agree; but, as the story of
the infant baptism indicates, Christians have different commitments
regarding where in the church we find the Spirit's real work. Here I
turn to the practices of the church as a locus of the Spirit's work and
the church's public witness. I focus on two characteristics of practices
through which the Holy Spirit enacts its sanctifying mission. First, as
said above, they are public and visible. Second, they take their form
from Christ's own. Both characteristics are essential in the Spirit's
textually mediated witness to the nations.

In his essay *On the Councils and the Church*, Martin Luther asks
a question that could easily be asked today: "Where can a confused
person see the church in the world?" His answer is, "Wherever you *see*
the following practices taking place."[8] Luther presents seven "marks"
as constitutive of the church: the preaching and hearing of the Word,
baptism, the Lord's Supper, the office of the keys, ordination, prayer/
praise/catechism, and the way of the cross or Christian discipleship.[9]
Others speak of practices in a more expansive but not unlimited way.
For example, in *Practicing Our Faith* Dorothy Bass explores twelve
Christian practices from honoring the body to household economics.[10]
The seven practices Luther lists are all visible, public, and shared.
There is no secret knowledge or handshake. No insider trading. The
practices belong to the people, not to the clergy or the church hierar-
chy. The early church struggled with and rejected gnosticism—secret

8. Luther, *Luther's Works*, 41:148–68 (emphasis mine). Cf. Braaten and Jenson, *Marks of the Body of Christ*, vii–xii.
9. Braaten and Jenson, *Marks of the Body of Christ*, vii–xii.
10. See also Miroslav Volf and Dorothy Bass, *Practicing Theology*.

knowledge given to some and not others. It claimed that everything we need to know about God is passed down publicly from generation to generation, beginning with the prophets and apostles.

We often forget this and act as if what we do in church and how we behave isn't meant to be seen by others. Private worship exists, to be sure. Jesus teaches us to shut the door of our room and pray to our Father in secret (Matt. 6:6). But in every country, in every language, and in every conceivable sort of gathering place, what happens? On Sunday mornings, Saturday nights, Wednesday evenings, and early Thursday mornings? Doors are unlocked and lights are turned on; people gather in basements, under trees, and on beaches. Notices of all kinds, from word of mouth to crowdsourcing, tell people when services will take place. In some countries this means gathering in a place hidden from the authorities. All are welcome: the curious, the confused, and the person of another faith, along with those who have been part of the congregation since before they were born. All are invited to join in a shared service of worship. People read Scripture, preach, clap and sing, dance, baptize, practice hospitality, teach, reach out their hands for living bread, give generously, seek and offer forgiveness, and are sent out to do the same in their various worlds. Public worship is a visible response to God's universal reach. It is public because that reach is available to all.[11]

The public and shared practices of the church take their form (in all their particularity) from Christ. The church bears in its body the marks of Christ (Gal. 6:17). The specific practices are (as were Israel's) an embodiment of the one we have put ourselves in a position to be addressed by. Because they take their shape from Christ and are constitutive of the church, they are not of our design. The focus on outward practices is based on the conviction of Christ's transforming presence in the church and confidence in the Spirit's power to use external forms, such as preaching, liturgy, baptism, repentance, and sacrificial giving, to conform us to Christ. Why? Because these outward forms are themselves formed through the Holy Spirit by the external

11. In *Confessing Jesus Christ*, David Lose raises the concern that Campbell's homiletic approach, coming out of Lindbeck, cannot lead to personal trust in Jesus Christ. Here I argue that the practices of the church embody acts of personal trust as well as public actions. See Lose, *Confessing Jesus Christ*, 126.

Word. They are the eternal and public shape of Scripture's imprint on the church, the very shape of Christ himself. Augustine describes these practices as expressions of the divine economy—Scripture and preaching, baptism and Eucharist, all are means the Spirit uses to captivate the mind and heal the heart by reordering affections.[12]

For this reason, preaching is one practice in the church among many. As described in the introduction, clergy know that their church is an ecosystem of relationships and practices, and preaching finds its rightful place in this rich soil. Each practice takes its shape from Christ's life. Each is open to misunderstanding, distortion, and abuse. Each stands in need of being corrected by the proclamation and teaching of the gospel. Paul Scott Wilson wrestles with the question, "What is lost when preaching is unaccompanied by Holy Communion?"[13] He asks, for example, why in Reformed churches the strong tradition of preaching did not negate the need for the Eucharist or its great prayer.[14] In *Theology Is for Proclamation*, Gerhard Forde spells out the nature of proclamation in preaching, emphasizing Scripture as God's living word as "doing the text to the reader."[15] But in a brief chapter in *Marks of the Body of Christ*, he points to its wider reach.[16] "Whereas proclamation is particularly focused in the preaching, it takes place abundantly elsewhere. The liturgy, of course, puts much proclamation on our lips and constrains us to do it even if we don't want to. The mutual consolation of brothers and sisters, the private exercise of the office of the keys, and so forth are prominent instances in which proclamation is to take place. The church leaves its mark when it proclaims."[17]

12. Kolbet, *Augustine and the Cure of Souls*, 194.

13. Paul Scott Wilson, "Preaching and the Sacrament of Holy Communion," in *Preaching in the Context of Worship*, ed. David M. Greenhaw and Ronald J. Allen (St. Louis: Chalice, 2000), 61. This article is an excellent review of preaching from a Reformed perspective.

14. P. Wilson, "Preaching and the Sacrament," 48.

15. Gerhard O. Forde, *Theology Is for Proclamation* (Minneapolis: Augsburg Fortress, 1990), 2. Forde is contrasting proclamation as information about the gospel with proclamation as present tense address, which demands a response from the listener. "The only appropriate response is likewise primary: confession, praise, prayer and worship. Proclamation as primary discourse demands an answer in like discourse be it positive or negative: 'I repent, I believe' or 'I don't, I won't, I can't.'"

16. Gerhard O. Forde, "The Word That Kills and Makes Alive," in Braaten and Jenson, *Marks of the Body of Christ*, 1–12.

17. Forde, "Word That Kills and Makes Alive," 6.

Luther insisted that the clarity of Scripture and its preaching depended on its place among the public and shared practices of the church. Scripture has both inward clarity and outward clarity. The inward clarity is located in the heart's understanding, which is solely the work of the Holy Spirit. Yeago quotes Martin Luther regarding the outward clarity, which is "'located in the ministry of the word' (*in verbi ministerio posita*), that is, in the network of ecclesial communicative practices within which both text and interpreter are situated."[18] Scripture's clarity is found within and through the church's many forms of proclamation: teaching, preaching, worship, catechesis, mission, and so on. Its clarity is neither separate from nor prior to the church's engagement with it.[19] Because practices are open to misunderstanding, distortion, and abuse, they need to be described and corrected by the proclamation and teaching of the gospel, and the proclamation of Scripture needs the enactment of the practices of the church for its outward clarity.

What Is Christ's Word about Us?

Proclaiming a shared identity which Christ gives us is difficult partly because of two adjectives that describe this identity: "received" and "shared." First, it is a received identity. God gives it to us in Jesus Christ; that is, we do not construct it. This received identity pertains to all persons. Thus, it is shared. "For just as the body is one and has many members, and all the members of the body, though many, are one body, so it is with Christ" (1 Cor. 12:12). Like the publican in the temple, we prefer to see ourselves as distinct from others (Luke 18:9–14). The identity we are given in Christ, however, cuts through our self-differentiation and self-congratulation. With Paul, who quotes the Psalter and Isaiah, we must say, "There is no one who is righteous, not even one; there is no one who has understanding, there is no one who seeks God" (Rom. 3:10–11). We proclaim this through the light of God's grace, knowing that Christ died for the ungodly: "For there is no distinction, since all have sinned and fall short of the glory of God; they

18. Yeago, "Bible: The Spirit, the Church and the Scriptures," 57.
19. Yeago, "Bible: The Spirit, the Church and the Scriptures," 58–59.

are now justified by his grace as a gift, through the redemption that is in Christ Jesus, whom God put forward as a sacrifice of atonement by his blood, effective through faith" (vv. 22–25). But, still, it is a hard sell, made more difficult as the preacher tries to find language that is shared by her congregation. Can a preacher use the language of our shared identity as "sinner" these days? Or as "ungodly"? Many stop listening. Turning to more therapeutic language for our shared identity, such as "broken" or "wounded," shuts the ears of others. Thus it is tempting to preach in individualist terms or in such general ways as to be inoffensive. But this is not sufficient. Question 5, What is Christ's word about us? is a reminder that preaching is about discerning the body—our own mortality, our ungodliness, Christ's marred and glorified body, and our shared yet difficult life in just this body.

Preaching: Discerning the Body as a Way of Life

In his first letter to the Corinthians, Paul describes the practice of receiving the Eucharist as a practice of discerning the body (1 Cor. 10:14–22; 11:17–34). His description helps us think about preaching also as a practice of discerning the body. Preaching as discerning the body involves recognizing, describing, receiving, and conforming to the body of Jesus, crucified and raised for us. This includes God's judgment on our failures to do this, as well as our repentance and amendment of life. I will take these in order.

Our identity is given in the Eucharist. "Because there is one bread, we who are many are one body, for we all partake of the one bread" (1 Cor. 10:17). Augustine's famous phrase is linked to the bread: "Become what you see, and receive what you are."[20] Yet when the Corinthians come together as the church, Paul writes that there are divisions among them (11:18). In 1 Corinthians 10 and 11, Paul addresses how their behavior degrades the Eucharistic meal, though their Christian identity ought to preclude this. "When you come together, it is not really to eat the Lord's Supper. For when the time comes to eat, each of you goes ahead with your own supper, and one goes hungry and another becomes drunk. What! Do you not have homes to eat and drink in?

20. Augustine, Sermon 272, "On the day of Pentecost—To the Catechumens, concerning the Sacrament," in *Essential Sermons*, 318.

Or do you show contempt for the church of God and humiliate those who have nothing?" (11:20–22). When Paul says in verse 20 that they have not really come together to eat the Lord's Supper, he is not speaking so much of the physical act of receiving the bread and wine but of a way of life. That way of life is participation in the Lord's body and blood (10:16–17). Paul sums up the connection between the gift of the Eucharist and the way of life that marks Christians and the church in the single phrase "discerning the body" (11:29).

Preaching is a practice in which we are called to discern the body as a way of life. Preaching, as Augustine described it, is an "audible sign" with bread and wine as "visible words."[21] In preaching we have the privilege of naming and describing the reality already present in the church as it gathers in the name of the risen Christ and breaks bread together. It is our privilege to describe the way of life springing from this reality.

In this fifth question we ask what Christ's address to us in his word says about us, that is, what God has made us to be and to become. We listen together with our congregation toward this end: to recognize what it means to participate in this way of life through the practices of the church and after we leave the physical gathering of the community. As preachers we cultivate our imaginations to do this in our particular contexts. The language of sermons—narratives, images, metaphors, stories, and examples—is well suited for this task. The Spirit uses the practice of preaching to renew our minds (Rom. 12:2) as we begin to recognize what Christ has already made us. Stories are one way, as we will see in the next chapter, to continue with the Spirit-led task of recognition. They help to answer the questions, What does participation in the body we have recognized look like? What does this way of life look like here and now?[22]

Preaching as discerning the body involves conforming to the body. In Paul's description of the call to discern the body in the Eucharist, he speaks of the way the Eucharist itself "judges" its participants (1 Cor.

21. See respectively, Robert W. Jenson, *Visible Words: The Interpretation and Practice of Christian Sacraments* (Philadelphia: Fortress, 1978), 4–5; Allan D. Fitzgerald, ed., *Augustine through the Ages: An Encyclopedia* (Grand Rapids: Eerdmans, 1999), 744.

22. Ellen F. Davis, *Imagination Shaped: Old Testament Preaching and the Anglican Tradition* (Valley Forge: Trinity Press International, 1995).

11:27–34). The Eucharist unveils the form of Christ, his subjection and
sacrificial love, and exposes to view the form of our own hearts. The
judgment we bring on ourselves by not discerning the body is in part
due to our misapprehension or rejection of Christ's form as our own.
As 1 Corinthians 11:30 says, "For this reason many of you are weak
and ill, and some have died."

Scripture, as the form of the crucified, self-giving Christ, witnesses
both to our unity in Christ and to our failures, divisions, corruption,
and violence. Thus the Spirit uses Scripture to form the church and to
correct and judge it, as the Spirit did with divided Israel. Most of the
church has always understood itself as a mixed bag, a *corpus mixtum*,
weeds and wheat that grow up together. The Spirit's use of Scripture
to continue to reform the church is a principle of many Reformed
churches. The following phrase (sometimes misquoted) first appeared
in 1674 in a devotional by Jodocus van Lodenstein, who was an important figure in the Dutch Reformed Church during the Dutch Second Reformation: "The church is reformed and always [in need of]
being reformed according to the Word of God." The overall shape of
the Articles of Religion of the Anglican Church makes clear that the
mediating forms of divine life, revealed in Christ through the Old and
New Testaments, shape the necessary response to the church's innate
fallibility and human corruption.[23] Richard Hooker held to the notion
of human corruption, the fallibility of the church, and the need for
Scripture's cure: "How should our festered sores be cured, but that
God hath delivered a law as sharp as the two-edged sword, piercing
the very closest and most unreachable corners of the heart, which the
law of Nature hardly, human laws by no means possible, reach unto?"[24]

23. Article 21 enshrines coherence with "holy Scripture" as the only authoritative
template for the church, and article 20 focuses on this explicitly: "The Church hath power
to decree Rites or Ceremonies, and authority in Controversies of Faith: And yet it is not
lawful for the Church to ordain anything that is contrary to God's Word written, neither
may it so expound one place of Scripture, that it be repugnant to another. Wherefore,
although the Church be a witness and keeper of holy Writ, yet, as it ought not to decree
any thing against the same, so besides the same ought it not to enforce any thing to be
believed for the necessity of Salvation" (in *Book of Common Prayer*).

24. W. Speed Hill and Georges Edelen, eds., *Of the Laws of Ecclesiastical Polity:
Preface and Books I–IV*, vol. 1 of *The Folger Library Edition of the Works of Richard Hooker*
(Cambridge, MA: Harvard University Press, 1977), 12.1.

Repentance and Amendment of Life

Love turned in on itself, love closed off to our neighbor, love that will not spend itself for others does not last, but fades, sickens, and ultimately dies. Such is Scripture's witness and Paul's testimony. Can our failures in our sermons to discern and describe the body as a way of life lead to such dissipation? The act of discerning the body leads to repentance, which is a form of recognition. We acknowledge before God and neighbor how far short we are of who God has made us, and we ask God's mercy and forgiveness. We do so confident in Christ's transforming presence in the church and in the Spirit's power through preaching, liturgy, baptism, repentance, sacrificial giving, and other practices. These conform us to Christ. In a sense these outward forms are the eternal and public shape of Scripture's imprint on the church, the very shape of Christ himself. If we do not preach about who we are in Christ, we withhold the invitation to both recognition and repentance. We quite literally leave our people to wander about in their misapprehensions. We are called to do more.

"We" Is a Personal Pronoun: Practices for Recognizing Our Corporate Identity

A light hand, not a heavy hammer, is the tool for describing our shared identity in sermons and our failures to discern the body. Glimpses, snapshots, hints, renderings that stir the imagination and begin to invite (not coerce) a congregation to think about themselves in a new way—these will invite both recognition and repentance. Images may come both from Scripture and from our own imaginations. For example, Margaret Silf in *Landmarks*, a book on Ignatian spirituality, tells of a church potluck at which all the food was gone but one salad. The parishioners realized why: someone had forgotten to include a serving spoon. The church is often like that, Silf reports. People are hungry and longing to eat, but where is the spoon?[25] Recognition and repentance.

It takes the full, complex life, activity, and organization of Christian people around the world, formed in and by Christ, to begin to recognize

25. As told in Craig G. Bartholomew and David J. H. Beldman, *Hearing the Old Testament: Listening for God's Address* (Grand Rapids: Eerdmans, 2012), xv.

and inhabit this unity. In the ecosystem of the church, the sermon is only one practice through which the unity we share in Christ is interpreted, named, and made visible. The weekly round of preaching is well suited for this slow process of renewing our minds through the Spirit because preaching is both repetitive and cumulative. Over time, how we hear Scripture changes. As Augustine said, we learn to listen together, to recognize that Christ addresses us together, to discover, as a colleague described it, that "we" is a personal pronoun.

Here are some questions we can use as tools to help us recognize the corporate identity God gives us in our local context. They are discipleship questions, not informational questions. They are questions about discerning the body as a way of life.

- How in this Scripture passage (and those around it) does God describe who he has made the church to be?
  - ▶ With our sisters and brothers there?
  - ▶ With himself?
  - ▶ With our failures and sins?
  - ▶ With the future?
  - ▶ With creation?
  - ▶ With those who do not know him?
  - ▶ With the disobedient world?
- As God addresses us in this Scripture, how does God name and describe the vocation of the church and its role in his mission?
- In his word to us in this Scripture, how does God describe our identity as witnesses, individually and corporately?
- In this Scripture, how does God describe our congregation in terms of our relationship with each other, our neighborhood, and his mission?
- What does God say about our visible, shared way of life?

The Preacher as Theologian of a Broken Body

Many who consider themselves to be outside the church, and indeed many parishioners, can best recognize the church by its failures, shortcomings, divisions, arguments, and abuses. Is it possible to speak of a shared identity to those who have been harmed by the church? Can we speak of a shared identity that does not divide people into insiders and outsiders? George Sumner, a former principal of Wycliffe College, describes the church as a place of "faith and holiness mixed with human confusion and grasping, like those wheat and tares in Jesus' parable."[26] Yet in the face of this flawed reality, Sumner goes on to say that "even in the chapel of the Kingdom of heaven, the Church is a cracked clay pot in which the jewel of the Gospel is found."[27] It is found there because Christ is there. Our participation in the fellowship of the Trinity and the saints—the unity that is the Spirit's testimony to the nations—is only made possible by Jesus Christ, who incorporates us into himself in his body. "For his Church he knoweth and loveth, so that they which are in the Church are thereby known to be *in him*."[28] Calvin describes this as the mystical union. Paul describes this reality of being "in Christ" over seventy times in his letters. When Jesus speaks of himself, he refuses to distance himself from his body, despite its failures. "Saul, Saul, why do you persecute me?" he asked, to which Saul answered, "Who are you, Lord?" The reply came, "I am Jesus, whom you are persecuting. But get up and enter the city, and you will be told what you are to do" (Acts 9:4–6). The Jesus whom Saul is persecuting is, of course, Jesus's followers, who are his body.

Our Reformation roots remind us that the church both proclaims and distorts the gospel. The preacher, as theologian and pastor, needs to remember this and speak of the identity we are given in Christ with humility and honesty. Our ability to speak of a shared identity lies in the promise that judgment begins with the church (1 Pet. 4:17). In the face of the church's many failures and abuses, silence or withdrawal is not our only option. Just as God never left divided Israel, Christ has not withdrawn from the church. Christ turns to her and judges her. Repentance is perhaps the greatest power Christ gives the church. It is our response to the call to discern the body, the tangled flesh with its promises and reality. We can repent of squandering Christ's life and light because he stands among us even in our sin and waits for

26. George Sumner, *Wycliffe College Handbook* (Toronto: Wycliffe College, 2010), 6.
27. Sumner, *Wycliffe College Handbook*, 6.
28. Hill and Edelen, *Laws of Ecclesiastical Polity: Book V*, 56.7 (emphasis mine).

our confession. He is the head of his torn, flaccid body, which refuses to use its mind and strength for his work in the world. We repent and open our hands to receive his grace and mercy for the amendment of our common life. Repentance is the witness the church bears to the nations at this time. We have good news to preach.

From Witness to Confessor to Theologian: Jesus and Mary in the Garden

The story of Mary meeting her risen Lord in the garden after his resurrection points to the movement of the preacher from witness to confessor to theologian of the body (John 20:11–18). In the relationship between Mary, the risen Jesus, and the disciples, we see the movement between personal and corporate address, and between personal and corporate identity; and we see tension between personal experience and the vocation of preaching. At the least, this story names *as one vocation* the privilege of being both hearers and preachers of God's Word, among and for God's people.

Mary has come to anoint a body. Christ's creaturely and bodily existence extends beyond his death. She does not recognize the risen Jesus until he addresses her personally. When he asks her, "Woman, why are you weeping?" she thinks he is the gardener. When he says to her, "Mary," she turns to him and says, "Rabbouni." Here in Jesus's personal address to Mary, we see our vocation to listen for Jesus's word addressed to each of us. We also see the ongoing dialectic between address and identity. This story turns on Christ's personal address to Mary and her response. But she did not go to the tomb to listen for such an address. She went to anoint the body of a dead friend. That is, her identity as friend and disciple led her to his tomb this Easter morning, where, unwittingly, she puts herself in a position to be addressed by the one who calls to her because he is alive.

Jesus's directive to Mary points to the role of the preacher as theologian of a broken body. After Mary recognizes her risen Savior, he tells her to go to his friends and tell them this: "I am ascending to my Father and your Father, to my God and your God" (John 20:17). Jesus describes the identity he has given her and the other disciples in his resurrection: my Father, *your* Father, my God, *your* God. Jesus reaches across the biblically defined chasm of otherness between God and God's creation and invites the first disciples and us into the identity he shares with his Father. To Mary he describes who he has made us to be.

As the story concludes, we see the call and challenge to hold on to our personal experience of the risen Lord's address to us while simultaneously moving beyond it in the practice of proclamation.[29] Jesus tells Mary what to preach. He does not send her to his friends to speak primarily of her personal experience of their conversation outside his empty tomb. "Go to my brothers and say to them, 'I am ascending to my Father and your Father, to my God and your God'" (20:17). He sends her to tell them of his resurrection and ascension, of his identity, so to speak. Mary does both. John writes that "Mary Magdalene went and announced to the disciples, 'I have seen the Lord'; and she told them that he had said these things to her" (v. 18).

If John had included Mary's homily to the other disciples in his Gospel (as Luke includes Peter's in Acts 3), we would have a model of what it looks like to move from God's personal address to God's word to the church. But we do have this story, in which Jesus addresses Mary personally and then sends her to her friends to tell of his identity as the risen and ascended Christ and of their identity in him. This alone is encouragement for the practice of preaching.

---

29. We can hear Jesus's command to Mary, "Do not hold on to me," as the directive not to hold on to our personal experience of him exclusively.

6

QUESTION 6

"What Does It Look Like?"

The Preacher as Witness to Christ
in a Disobedient World

▶ **Main action:** Facilitate recognition of how the identity of Christ is
inhabited in a broken and disobedient world.

My sermon preparation in the parish followed a standard weekly
rhythm. I'd spend Monday mornings in the office mopping up from
Sunday: writing welcome notes to newcomers, attending to pastoral
concerns that had come to my attention, and so on. Monday afternoons
I'd begin to prepare for midweek Bible studies or discipleship classes
and make any necessary hospital visits. Monday evenings I turned to
next Sunday's sermon. After dinner, while our kids did their homework,
I did mine. I read the assigned lessons, read around in the Scriptures,
and did the background work of question 1, which means giving Scripture the attentiveness it deserves. As I read, studied, and pondered, I
found that an image, a question, a word—something—captured my
imagination, which narrowed my focus. I then began to chew on question 2, Whom do I see? I'd put the Scripture and my sermon in the

oven to bake, so to speak, as I got ready for bed and went about the next day. It is a mysterious process of creation that as we go about our day, take walks, drive kids, shower, and travel from A to B, things are coming together and taking form in a way that is beyond the cognitive process. This creative process is, perhaps, a divinely sanctioned form of multitasking. On Wednesday afternoons I took my sermon out of the oven, tried to write a first draft, and then put it back in until Thursday evening or Friday morning when I tweaked it. If I was lucky, somewhere along the way a story would pop into my head, often while driving or working out at the gym. I was grateful every time.

What is the function of stories in a sermon? Entertainment, example, application, something a congregation will remember? In a theologically shaped practice of preaching, this is an important question to ask. This question contains three subquestions, which are addressed below. What is the relationship between the stories we tell, the Scripture on which we preach, and the Christ who addresses us in it? What is the theological and cultural weight of these stories? What is their relationship to the preachers who select and narrate them? These questions might make it seem daunting to use stories in sermons. Most preachers are simply grateful, as I was, that a story comes to mind. But this relief that with a story in hand the sermon is on its way often includes unease about the stories we tell.

The answer is not to ban stories in sermons. Our preaching means nothing if our communities do not believe that the risen Christ speaks to us today. Our preaching is for nothing if we do not proclaim this. It can also amount to nothing if we do not help our congregations learn with us to listen for God's Word and to recognize Christ at work in the hours and days of our lives and world. Ricoeur's claim that the absolute is always tied to narrated events is good news for preachers.[1] Sermon stories are essential. We don't need to throw them out completely.

We do need, however, to ask about their function and limitations. Question 6, What does it look like? is a reminder to do just this. It also suggests an answer. Sermon stories, like Scripture, witness to Christ. They can function like a beam of light illuminating Christ, to whom their narrated events are a response. Sermon stories can describe what

---

1. Ricouer, "Hermeneutics of Testimony," 133.

we look like in the Spirit's hands as the Spirit's witness to the nations. Thus, with this final question, the preacher comes full circle. Once again, she takes up the role of witness to what is or has already happened. Here she is a witness with a clear purpose: to look for and bring to light the face of Christ, hidden in stories large and small, ordinary and extraordinary.

Stories as Application, Expression, or Recognition? Crossing the Bridge between Scripture and Our Worlds

How does the preacher connect the Scripture, these old texts, to her setting—that is, to new ears—in a particular time and place? Questions of connection or correlation are central in biblical interpretation and homiletic theory. Frequently in homiletic theory the image used to describe the correlation of Scripture to the current time is a bridge. For example, John Stott's *Between Two Worlds* develops the image of preaching as bridge building.[2] Paul Scott Wilson aptly states that the bridge image evinces a connection.[3] But there is no agreement on just what that connection is. Walter Brueggemann makes just this point: "We have no methodological consensus about how to move from 'then' to 'now,' or even if it is legitimate to make the move. . . . The move very much depends on the interpreter's judgment about the needs and prospects of the present situation, a judgment inevitably personal."[4]

The image of the bridge is helpful for exploring the function of stories and their relationship to both Scripture and one's context. How we move from one to the other, as Brueggemann says, depends on the interpreter's judgments. First, bridges imply distance. There is a distance to be covered from one side to the other, whether it is from Fort Erie, Ontario, to Buffalo, New York, or from Paul, Isaiah, and Ruth to you and me and our counterparts in Tokyo and Tanzania. Second, a bridge declares that the distance can be traveled. Whether by foot, truck, bike, boat, or donkey, we can go from the US to Canada or from Corinth to Colorado. Preachers know that God is the only one

2. John R. W. Stott, *Between Two Worlds: The Art of Preaching in the Twentieth Century* (Grand Rapids: Eerdmans, 1982).

3. Paul Scott Wilson, *Preaching and Homiletical Theory* (St. Louis: Chalice, 2004), 50.

4. As quoted in P. Wilson, *Preaching and Homiletical Theory*, 35.

who can bridge this gap, and yet preachers also know they still have a role. Stories are one way we do so. How we use them in this journey is shaped by how we interpret the distance we need to travel.

In preaching there are three main ways to bridge this gap: through application, a universal shared experience, and the continuum of the church.[5] Each is erected on a different understanding of Scripture and how it travels through time. Application is a hallmark of expository preaching. Like most aspects of preaching, there is lively conversation about its contours, the need for it, and the role of the preacher vis-à-vis the Holy Spirit.[6] Application is based on the conviction that the preacher's task involves more than explaining Scripture. It includes helping people to live Scripture in concrete ways. Generally, in expository preaching the preacher starts on one side of the bridge with Scripture. Through historical, critical, and literary analysis of the text, the preacher unearths its truths and carries those truths across the bridge to the other side where her parishioners live and wait. "Application in the expository sermon is the process whereby the expositor takes a biblical truth of the text and applies it to the lives of his audience, proclaiming why it is relevant for their lives, practically showing how it should affect their lives, and passionately encouraging them to make the necessary changes in their lives in a manner congruent with the original intent of the author."[7] Application involves more than using sermon illustrations or stories. It involves examples, practical suggestions, and exhortation. Whatever form it takes, it rests on the conviction that biblical truths are transportable across time and are meant to be implemented. The preacher, with the help of the Holy

5. This description is loosely based on George Lindbeck's taxonomy of the uses of doctrine. Lindbeck aims to offer an alternative to liberal theology by questioning the role of correlation in theology. Lindbeck presents three models and argues for the third. The three types are (1) a cognitive-propositional model in which doctrine functions as informative propositions or truth claims about objective realities, (2) an experiential-expressive model in which doctrine functions as nondiscursive symbols that can change meaning, and (3) a cultural-linguistic model in which doctrine functions as authoritative rules of discourse the way grammar functions in language. See Lindbeck, *Nature of Doctrine*, 1–34.

6. For a thorough overview of various arguments for and against the need for application, see Hershael W. York and Scott A. Blue, "Is Application Necessary in Expository Preaching?," *Southern Baptist Journal of Theology* 7 (Summer 1999): 70–84.

7. York and Blue, "Is Application Necessary?," 73–74.

Spirit—or the Holy Spirit with the help of the preacher—carries these truths to parishioners for practical application. In a sense, application tries to answer the question the crowds at the Jordan asked John the Baptist after he proclaimed a gospel of repentance to them: "What then should we do?" (Luke 3:10).

Preaching that is considered liberal also works according to a bridge model. But what is considered true across time in "liberal" preaching is different from what is considered true in expository preaching.[8] What is true and endures is not necessarily a biblical truth but a universal human experience of the transcendent across time, space, and culture. The preacher's task is to unearth these religious experiences embedded in the language of Scripture and carry them across the bridge to where parishioners live and wait. Here the preacher's task of transportation often includes translation. Scripture is only one language that expresses these truths and is not always the most helpful. The preacher's task is to find the contemporary language that will express this experience, and the congregation will nod their heads in recognition.

Both expository and "liberal" approaches, different as they are, assume that Scripture can speak to the lives of parishioners *and* that it is somehow outside of those lives. In expository preaching the preacher assumes that Scripture needs to be applied. Liberal approaches carry hope that it can be translated into a contemporary context. In both approaches there is something to be extracted from the text—a biblical truth or a universal human experience of the transcendent. A question to ask about both approaches is, What happens to the text of Scripture once the truth or universal experience has been extracted? Is it left on the far side of the bridge? In both approaches the burden of making an old text relevant today is placed on the preacher's shoulders.

This theologically shaped practice of preaching begins with a different starting place, not on the far side of the bridge with the job of transporting goods to the other side. Scripture is not on the far side

8. Liberal theology, for the purpose of this discussion, is the theological movement traced to the early nineteenth-century German Enlightenment, characterized by its emphasis on a historical-critical method, which deemphasizes the narrative presentation of the faith and the role of the community in interpretation. Liberal theology sought a referent outside of Scripture, frequently a kind of universal experience. The apologetic goal of liberal theology was to relate the meaningfulness of Christian faith and Scripture to a general human experience.

nor is it outside the lives of people today. Scripture speaks directly into parishioners' lives because in it the living, ascended Christ, the Son of the God of Israel, addresses us as he did Lydia, Job, Barnabas, the Syrophoenician woman, and every generation since. God's address forms a single people across all time who, in the Spirit's hands, are God's witness to the nations through their common life. We are as much a part of Scripture—or as Robert Jenson describes it, "*inside the story Scripture tells*"—as any of them.[9] "Acts 29" churches, a self-described family of church-planting churches, points to this same idea. The church across time is a single continuum, whose life itself is an interpretation of Scripture. This commitment shapes all six questions of sermon preparation, including this final one on the use of stories.

This claim changes the distance between text and people and the preacher's task, and thus renders the bridge model of preaching unhelpful. To be sure, a historical distance spans the fixed text of Scripture and today's people. But an understanding of the single community across time, of which we are a part, gets the preacher out of the transportation and translation business and into the business of listening with her congregation to the address of the living God. It eases the burden on the preacher's shoulders of making Scripture relevant. Jesus Christ is inherently relevant. The commitment to Scripture as the single address to the church across time roots the preacher's vocation not in extracting goods from the text to transport to her congregation, but in developing with them the practices of attentiveness, listening, and recognition of the one who addresses us there.

Understanding that the Spirit uses Scripture to form the church as a single, continuous community across time who can hear and respond to God's Word does not collapse the centuries. There are, for example, historical distances between divided Israel, the struggles in the church in Corinth, and our divided churches. The knowledge that Scripture is the single address to the church across time shapes how we use these exegetical tools. Jenson describes the tools of historical-critical and literary analysis as valuable servants of this larger reality and the practices of attending, listening, and recognition.

9. Jenson, "Scripture's Authority in the Church," in Davis and Hays, *Art of Reading Scripture*, 30.

This does not mean that the historical-critical labors are futile or unnecessary. The story told by Scripture has been in progress for millennia, and *within it* there are historical distances in plenty, and so, in the narrative of this history, hermeneutical gaps in plenty. I do indeed need to build exegetical bridges between, say, Moses and Paul or between Paul and myself. But there is no gap to be bridged between the unitary community of interpretation from which these documents come and in which we now work at reading them, since these are not two communities of interpretation but only one.[10]

If the bridge model is unhelpful in this theological vocation, how should we reenvision the task of spanning this distance? An image used by various theologians to describe our relationship to Scripture is that of a play or a book. Hans Frei, relying on Erich Auerbach's work, describes Scripture as a realistic narrative.[11] Jenson describes it as a play or drama.[12] We are characters in the play whose author and main character is God. It is the drama of God with his creation and of God's own life as Father, Son, and Holy Spirit. It tells the story of a continuous community, which includes its authors, who formed the books that became the canon of Scripture for future generations. As such, we are characters who are in the rare position of having read the preceding chapters or acts, where God's character and our character or identity in relationship to God and creation have been established. We continue the drama in a new set of circumstances, but the acts or chapters that have come before are determinative of the horizons of our actions. "If we are faithless, he remains faithful—for he cannot deny himself" (2 Tim. 2:13). For example, God's relationship with his fractured and divided church is a continuation of his relationship with divided Israel. Our struggles with idolatry in all its contemporary forms are a continuation of the same struggle that has plagued our forebears since act 1.

Since the people of God are in Scripture rather than outside it, preaching is an act of continuation more than correlation. What we

10. Jenson, "Scripture's Authority in the Church," 31.
11. Frei, *Eclipse of Biblical Narrative*; see also chap. 1 of Erich Auerbach, *Mimesis: The Representation of Reality in Western Literature*, trans. Willard R. Trask (Princeton: Princeton University Press, 1968).
12. Jenson, "Scripture's Authority in the Church," 32–33.

bring to our people is not something we have extracted from Scripture—a biblical truth, a bit of wisdom, a universal experience. We bring to our people the shared task of attentiveness to Scripture, listening together to the one we meet there, the one who addresses us in it and has created us to carry on the story in our time and place. Our communities, as a part of the larger church, are the fundamental form of the interpretation of Scripture. Our communities, in their local and cultural particularity, bound to their neighbor and God's mission, witness to our response to the one who addresses us. Like the seven churches in the beginning of the revelation to John, our witness seems too often to point to the church's failures (Rev. 2:1–3:22): its silence in the face of great evil and suffering, its failures to commend the faith to others, its love of wealth. But even here the measuring rod of the church's witness is Jesus Christ, Son of the God of Israel, who died and rose to set the world right. Christ is always our true north, our lodestone. Thus, when we interpret stories of the church's faithfulness and of its failures (and name them as such) we can witness to Jesus Christ. Sermon stories are an opportunity to do just this.

The Good News and the Bad News about Stories: The Limits of Narrative

The good news about the use of stories in sermons, as said above, is that they are needed. We don't need to throw them out completely. The bad news is that they cannot do everything we think or hope they can. It is the preacher's task to assess their limits and their purpose in the pulpit. Scripture as a single canon is helpful for doing so. Its variety of literary genres woven together forms the fixed text through which God addresses us and through which the Spirit forms a people capable of hearing, responding, and being its witness to the nations. Our faith rests on this single story; we are formed as a people through it and are indeed part of it. But narrative per se, or plot per se, is not privileged in Scripture in the way we have come to believe and depend on in the pulpit. Storytelling is not the only way to express the experience of faith.

We come by our prolific use of stories, and a definition of preaching as storytelling, honestly. Narrative preaching and story as a primary vehicle to communicate the gospel dominated the pulpits of North

America for many decades, beginning in the 1970s. In the movement known as the New Homiletic, Fred Craddock, Eugene Lowry, Charles Rice, and others sought to revitalize the preaching ministry of the church by rescuing it from its long-standing bondage to an Aristotelian frame of reference and its more recent captivity to the world behind the text.[13] This rescue operation is now taken for granted, but at the time it was considered a homiletical bombshell, changing the basic pattern of preaching in North America and dominating the preaching literature for the next thirty years.

The New Homiletic turned to the narrative form of Scripture, the narrative quality of experience, and the eventfulness of the Word. It redefined the form of the sermon, the place of the listener, and the authority and role of the preacher. In it the preacher's task is to deliver the eventful experience of the Word. The preacher can deliver this experience in various ways, such as replicating the form of Scripture in the form of her sermon, in the delivery of her own experience, or in the delivery of the experience in a story, film, or play.[14] Because the New Homiletic is based on the universal nature of the narrative quality of experience, the preacher can best serve the gospel with her own story and experience—what she *is* here and now, which points beyond what we are here and now.[15] The preacher's authority rests in her humanity.

This bombshell settled into the landscape of North American preaching, and preaching's turn to the subject provided fertile soil for the rise of postmodern homiletics. Exegeting one's context, feminist homiletics, Latin American Liberation Theology, and African American preaching are heirs to the New Homiletic and are its choice fruits.[16] At the same

13. George Bass, "The Evolution of the Story Sermon," *Word & World* 2, no. 2 (1982): 183–89. See also Edmund Steimle, Morris Niedenthal, and Charles Rice, *Preaching the Story* (Philadelphia: Fortress, 1980); Charles Rice, "The Preacher as Storyteller," *Union Seminary Quarterly Review* 31 (Spring 1976): 182–97; Eugene Lowry, *The Homiletical Plot: The Sermon as Narrative Art Form* (Louisville: Westminster John Knox, 1980); David Buttrick, *Homiletic: Moves and Structures* (Philadelphia: Fortress, 1988).

14. See Rice, "Preacher as Storyteller."

15. Rice, "Preacher as Storyteller," 33.

16. Ronald J. Allen, *Preaching and the Other: Studies of Postmodern Insights* (St. Louis: Chalice, 2009); Brian Blount and Lenora Tubbs Tisdale, eds., *Making Room at the Table: An Invitation to Multicultural Worship* (Louisville: Westminster John Knox, 2001); Walter J. Burghardt, SJ, *Hear the Just Word and Live It* (New York: Paulist Press, 2000); Charles L. Campbell, *The Word before the Powers: An Ethic of Preaching* (Louisville: Westminster

time, without negating the many contributions of the New Homiletic, some began to question the limits of narrative preaching, the narrative quality of experience, and whether preaching as an event is too individualistic.[17] By the mid-1990s a few homileticians began to call for a change in the subject of preaching, away from the listener and back to God.[18] Paul Scott Wilson, Will Willimon, and Thomas Long were early voices.[19]

What are the limits of what story can do? Richard Lischer describes four characteristics of the genre of story that limit its usefulness in preaching: aesthetic, ontological, theological, and social-political.[20] The aesthetic nature of stories lulls us into believing that something about the freestanding narrative form renders them inherently able to proclaim the gospel. Their meaning is self-referential and easily accessible. All we need to do is tell a story, and our congregations will intuitively or organically get what its plot conveys, exemplifies, or illustrates. Confidence in the aesthetic nature of stories can lull preachers into believing that they do not need to be interpreted. Yet all the stories in Scripture, from prehistory to parables, are part of something bigger, which

John Knox, 2002); Justo L. González and Catherine G. González, *The Liberating Pulpit* (Nashville: Abingdon, 1994); Cleophus James LaRue, *The Heart of Black Preaching* (Louisville: Westminster John Knox, 2000); William B. McClain, *Come Sunday: The Liturgy of Zion* (Nashville: Abingdon, 1990); John McClure, *The Roundtable Pulpit: Where Leadership and Preaching Meet* (Nashville: Abingdon, 1995); Henry H. Mitchell, *Black Preaching: The Recovery of a Powerful Art* (Nashville: Abingdon, 1990); Lucy A. Rose, "Conversational Preaching: A Proposal," *Journal for Preachers* 19, no. 1 (Advent 1995): 26–30; Lucy A. Rose, *Sharing the Word: Preaching in the Roundtable Church* (Louisville: Westminster John Knox, 1997); Christine Smith, *Preaching as Weeping, Confession, and Resistance: Radical Responses to Radical Evil* (Louisville: Westminster John Knox, 1992); Christine Smith, *Weaving the Sermon: Preaching in a Feminist Perspective* (Louisville: Westminster John Knox, 1989); Lenora Tubbs Tisdale, *Preaching as Local Theology and Folk Art* (Minneapolis: Fortress, 1997).

17. Richard Lischer, "The Limits of Story," *Interpretation* 38, no. 1 (1984): 26–38; Paul Scott Wilson, "Preaching at the Beginning of a New Millennium: Learning from Our Predecessors," *Journal for Preachers* 20, no. 4 (Pentecost 1997): 3–8. See, for example, Bryan Chapell, "When Narrative Is Not Enough," *Presbyterian* 22, no. 1 (1996): 3–16.

18. P. Wilson, *Preaching and Homiletical Theory*, 93.

19. William Willimon, "Postmodern Preaching: Learning to Love the Thickness of the Text," *Journal for Preachers* 19, no. 3 (Easter 1996): 32–37; Thomas G. Long, *Preaching from Memory to Hope* (Louisville: Westminster John Knox, 2009), xiii, 1–26.

20. Lischer, "Limits of Story," 29, 34. See also Chapell, "When Narrative Is Not Enough," 3–16.

provides a frame for our interpretation. The church never thought the story of God's relationship with creation was self-referential or that it did not need interpretation. The Epistles, which take the story of Israel and the crucified and risen Christ as their substructure, do just this.

The aesthetic nature of stories has also led us to believe that plot is more important than character. Stories have a beginning, middle, and end, a plot that moves from complication to resolution. While stories may be easy to tell and to remember—and sermon stories are what congregations most often remember—Lischer argues that to impose this structure on all experience distorts and even falsifies the way things are for many people. It misses the emptiness, anarchy, and despair of many lives. For example, we might ask, What is the plot of Aleppo or Mosul today? To what happy ending can this tragic situation lead? Thus, the limits of story are also ontological. Stories that tie everything together provide a sense of desperately needed order, but they also present a flawed view of the human person. The church, more than other organizations, endeavors to come alongside people whose lives fit no narrative plot, people who have reached a dead end rather than a resolution.

The limits of story are also theological. God breaks into our lives in all sorts of ways, disrupting the plotlines, or perhaps, for the first time, giving us an identity rooted in the larger story of his promises. God's ongoing grace, life, and mission do not work according to the normative form of story. Resurrection does not follow Christ's death because the plot requires resolution. Christ's resurrection is not following the plotline of winter's movement into spring, as more than one preacher has announced. God's action in raising Christ negates the old story and disrupts the narrative. The eschatological nature of the faith we are given cautions the preacher against relying on a strict narrative form of exposition.

Finally, the genre is better suited for cultural accommodation than for social-political change. Stories do not allow for the kind of ethical, social, and theological reflection necessary to live as God's people. A story about a polar bear stranded on a melting ice floe can inspire and even provide a sense of urgency. To become a vehicle for change, however, the story must be interpreted. Lischer writes that the effectiveness of Martin Luther King Jr. "as both a preacher and agent of social

change lay not in his ability to tell a story but in his incisive analysis of
the situation in America and his prophetic call to justice."[21] Theology
lives by story, but without precise modes of conceptualizing and interpreting these stories, theology is reduced to repetition or recital and
loses its power and its flexibility to address new situations. By asking
how stories function in sermons we acknowledge the possibilities and
limits of the genre and consider how to use stories judiciously. Stories
don't need to be thrown out but put in their proper place.

Showing Up in Our Sermons: The Bridge between My Story and Your Story, and My Story and *the* Story

How can the preacher be present in her sermons without continually
resorting to stories about her own experience? Is it only a matter of
proportion? My husband and I joke that it is time to move to a new
parish when he has told all his stories about being a missionary in
Burundi. However, to say that sermons should avoid personal stories
can lead unwittingly to the preacher exiting her own sermons. I was
talking with a colleague about a recent graduate from the seminary
where I work, who now serves in his parish. This young graduate is a
bright, serious, theologically informed pastor who is seeking new ways
of communicating the gospel to his generation. "His sermons are good,"
my colleague said, "very serious, but there is nothing of him in them."
We both agreed that the solution is not stories about his dog's illness
or sitting in the fair-trade café with his laptop, Bible, clerical collar, and
decaf Americano. "It's not his delivery or lack of content," my colleague
went on to explain, "but he never speaks about how the gospel engages
him, why it is true for him. In a sense he never shows up."

Can we use stories to show up in our sermons? Not as easily as
we wish we could. They cannot be the primary or only way we speak
of how the gospel engages us. They are not the shortcut around the
disciplined work of theological reflection we hope they can be. Experience is not universal, and our personal stories do not necessarily connect with others' experiences as we hope. The 2016 US presidential
election reminded us of this hard truth. The distance between the

---

21. Lischer, "Limits of Story," 35.

experiences of Americans is wider than we realized and more varied than we want to believe.

Repurposing the bridge model of preaching here will mark the distance between my story and yours. We want a shared or universal notion of experience to be the bridge spanning my story and yours. This well-meaning mistake is made in pastoral care as well as preaching. A parishioner is telling us about some difficult experience, and we interrupt to tell the story of a parallel experience—a similar car accident, our parent with cancer. We step out of their story into our own or another's in an attempt to show them that we understand their story. Most of the time it doesn't work. Counterintuitive though this seems, as Lischer states, "that story inevitably turns away from others and inward toward the self can be documented with an embarrassing degree of precision not only from the literature but also from the extensive use of first-person narration to which congregations are subjected on a typical Sunday morning."[22] By using our stories to connect with others, we've tried to cross the distance between ourselves and others on an unsteady bridge.

Can we learn from other people's experience? Can it be used by preachers to proclaim Jesus Christ? Yes! If not, we, our families, congregations, cities, and nations would be doomed to the passage of time as a repetition of the past. However, the experiences of others need to be interpreted. They need to be appropriated to point to and name what is embedded in and beyond their narrated events. The theologian Mary McClintock Fulkerson agrees: "Experience is not the *origin* of theology in the sense of the evidence for our claims, but the reality that needs to be explained."[23] This is how the Christian story has been received to create and sustain faith as it passes from generation to generation. Similarly, Lischer continues, "The same faculty that enables Christians to experience and express the world as duration also enables them to abstract, to generalize, to isolate images, all for the purpose of creating a formal structure of faith and life in the present."[24]

We do not need to, nor should we, download stories or turn to books

22. Lischer, "Limits of Story," 35.

23. Mary McClintock Fulkerson, *Changing the Subject: Women's Discourses and Feminist Theology* (Eugene, OR: Wipf and Stock, 1994), viii.

24. Lischer, "Limits of Story," 34.

of sermon examples or applications. It is the preacher's task to interpret stories. The question is, how and through what lens? How we use
stories depends, in part, on their function. Here I propose that a key
function of sermon stories is not unlike the function of Scripture itself.
Stories can witness to the Christ revealed in Scripture, as recognized
and responded to by the people in the story.

Stories as Witness: Seeing Others Love God Back

In this final question, What does it look like? the preacher again takes
up the role of witness or testifier. Here, her witness is not primarily
to what or to whom she sees in Scripture. Instead, through her use of
stories she tries to witness to Jesus *as recognized and responded to by the
participants in the story*. In a sense, whom the participants see and how
they respond to whom they see becomes a kind of text for the preacher.
Stories answer the questions, What does it look like to live as people
of God in this broken and disobedient world? What does it look like
to respond to God's love in Jesus Christ? The preacher and congregation together develop this essential Christian practice of recognition.

In one of her spiritual autobiographies, Anne Lamott writes that her
teenage son needs to see just this: to see in the actions of others their
love of God. She describes her insistence that her fourteen-year-old
son come to church with her and their negotiations over how often.

> We live in bewildering, drastic times, and a little spiritual guidance never
> killed anyone. I think it's a fair compromise that every other week he
> has to come to the place that has been the tap for me: I want him to see
> the people who have loved me when I felt most unlovable, who have
> loved him since I first told them that I was pregnant, even though he
> might not want to be with them. I want him to see their faces. He gets
> the most valuable things I know through osmosis. . . . And there are
> worse things for kids than to have to spend time with people who love
> God. Teenagers who do not go to church are adored by God, but they
> don't get to meet some of the people who love God back. Learning to
> love back is the hardest part of being alive.[25]

25. Anne Lamott, *Plan B: Further Thoughts on Faith* (New York: Riverhead Books,
2005), 195–96.

What does her insistence that her son come to church teach us about the use of stories in sermons? Sam, at age fourteen, knows a thing or two about God. In the first twelve years of his life, Sam and his mother probably missed church about ten times. Sam argues that he can spend time with God just as easily elsewhere as in church. His argument is one almost every parent has heard from their teenagers and every pastor has heard from adult parishioners. The variations of this argument reflect age, geography, and income. I can worship God at the beach, cottage, cabin, golf course, with my friends, hiking, or taking it easy after working the night shift. For Sam, it's hanging out with friends. His mother compromises but does not relent. She insists he come to church with her every other week. Lamott knows that God can find Sam anywhere. She knows that her son is adored by God and that Christ died for him. But it is at church that Sam gets to see people trying to love God back—and, as she says, this is not such a bad thing for any of us to see. Our ability to see what it looks like to love God back needs all the help we can get. Paul's declaration that our life is hidden with Christ (Col. 3:3) establishes the nature of this task of recognition: to develop the eyes to recognize what is hidden in plain sight. We need help learning to inhabit the identity we are given in Christ, with our failures, lukewarm attempts, and God's gracious and guiding response, in the ordinary and extraordinary moments of our lives and congregations. Preachers can help with this by how they interpret the stories they use in sermons. One kind of help is to interpret stories through this lens.

Scripture speaks of "seeing" the Word of God, that is, of a place, or perhaps a posture, where hearing and sight become one. It points to the possibility that listening can become sight. Isaiah saw the Word of the Lord that came to him concerning Judah and Jerusalem (Isa. 2:1); Habakkuk saw the oracle of God (Hab. 1:1). In Micah's day, the Word of the Lord came to Micah concerning Samaria and Jerusalem, and he not only heard it but saw it (Mic. 1:1). We point to this possibility in common speech: "Oh yes, now I see it," we say after struggling with something we didn't understand until finally it became clear. Is sight more durable than speech? The incarnation of the Word, Jesus Christ, has much to say about this question (John 1:14). Just as the Word spoken takes flesh in the incarnate Jesus so that the world may behold God's glory, so too Christ's address to us in Scripture must take flesh in the church through its common life and the lives of its members, gathered and dispersed. To use stories to witness to Christ, who is recognized and responded to by the story's participants, does more than illustrate how people try to love God back. William Shepherd, an Anglican homiletician, has said that our sermons help shape a community whose forms of life correspond to the patterns of Christ's life as received in Scripture.[26] Preaching joins other practices of the church, such as liturgy, in which Scripture's words take up, again and again, the task of learning to listen to, recognize, and respond to Christ, in the midst of our postmodern differences, as the Spirit reawakens and reorders love.

Lord, When Did We See You?

Scripture describes at least two ways people recognize and respond to Christ through the narrated events of their lives. The first occurs intentionally, though imperfectly, as belief leads to recognition and response. The second occurs without people knowing it until it has been interpreted to them. The first form of recognition springs from the promise Jesus makes to Martha at her brother's tomb: "Did I not tell you that if you believed, you would see the glory of God?" (John 11:40). The belief of the blind beggar, who calls Jesus "Son of David" and "Lord," leads to his ability to see Jesus (Luke 18:35–43): "Receive your sight; your faith has made you well" (v. 42 NASB). This first form, the sequence of belief leading to sight, is described as a source of encouragement in many of the epistles. The author of 1 Peter encourages the Christians dispersed in Asia Minor to hold on to this promise. "Although you have not seen him, you love him; and even though you do not see him now, you believe in him and rejoice with an indescribable and glorious joy, for you are receiving the outcome of your faith, the salvation of your souls" (1 Pet. 1:8–9).

Scripture also contains stories in which people respond to Christ without recognizing that they are doing so. The stories that take this

26. William Shepherd Jr., *No Deed Greater Than a Word: A New Approach to Biblical Preaching* (Lima, OH: CSS, 1998), 23; see also William Shepherd Jr., "A Rickety Bridge: Biblical Preaching in Crisis," *Anglican Theological Review* 80, no. 2 (1998): 186–206.

second form unveil two instructive truths for the preacher as she considers the function of stories in sermons. First, Scripture is clear that a lack of recognition does not negate the reality that the participant's actions are a response to Christ. Second, the lack of recognition moves to recognition through interpretation. Let me point to three such passages and take these two points in order. Saul did not recognize that when he threatened and bound the "people of the Way" he was threatening and binding Jesus (Acts 9:1–22). As described in the previous chapter of the present volume, the Christians in Corinth did not recognize that how they came together to eat bread and drink wine negated the body in which they were partaking (see 1 Cor. 11:17–32). In Matthew's description of the judgment of the nations, neither group recognizes that giving or withholding water, food, clothing, or visits is giving or withholding these things to or from Christ (Matt. 25:31–46). In all three passages the lack of recognition on behalf of the people involved does not negate the reality that their actions are a response to Christ.

Second, in all three passages someone witnesses to this reality, interprets it, so that the participants may see what is hidden in their actions. On the road to Damascus, Saul is only able to recognize this reality when the ascended Christ says to him, "I am Jesus, whom you are persecuting" (Acts 9:5). The Corinthian Christians have this reality exposed to them by Paul: "For all who eat and drink without discerning the body, eat and drink judgment against themselves" (1 Cor. 11:29). In the judgment of the nations, the nations recognize what was hidden in their actions only when the king answers them, "Truly I tell you, just as you did it to one of the least of these who are members of my family, you did it to me. . . . Just as you did not do it to one of the least, you did not do it to me" (Matt. 25:40, 45).

Our actions in the world, the narrated events of our lives—our stories—are the way we respond to Christ. They are how we try to love God back, whether intentionally though imperfectly, as belief leads to sight, or without recognizing it until it has been interpreted to us, or not at all, through our rejection of him. If Christ were just one of several forces in the world, one option among many, so to speak, then our actions could be considered in terms unrelated to him. Or only some of our actions could be considered as a response to him, intentional or unrecognized. Today I am trying to respond to Christ. Tonight I am not. But Christ is not one of many available forces in the world. This is God's world. God's own life creates it and holds it together each day. There is no world "outside" Christ, as we tend to think of it. Such is Scripture's witness.

Much of the time we, with our congregations, are like the disciples on the road to Emmaus on Easter morning (Luke 24:13–35). Christ is present as we go about our day, but our eyes are kept from recognizing him. Together with our congregations through Scripture, fellowship, and the breaking of bread, we can learn to recognize this marvelous truth. Kolbet argues that Augustine's goal for his preaching was "to keep the Christian congregation from being absorbed back into a world in which Christianity had by no means yet captured the cultural high ground."[27] He used preaching as a medium to try to pass on both the critical skills required to form a Christian identity and the constructive guidance necessary to sustain it. One of those critical skills is the ability to recognize our actions and those of others as a response to Christ, and not to something else. Sermon stories can help in the practice of recognition. Sermon stories, when interpreted, can function like a beam of light illuminating Jesus Christ, to whom their narrated events are a response.

Tools for Question 6

Any story we use in a sermon becomes our own in our telling of it, but this is not a license to interpret it to fit our needs. The knowledge that stories are always the narrator's construction should be a stern warning to the preacher for restraint. They are never culturally, theologically, and aesthetically neutral. No story will fit neatly into the functions I have described for them here. Stories, like life, are messy, incomplete, filled with our failures and shortcomings. To impose a narrative form on them, a beginning, middle, and end, is often just that—an imposition.

To interpret stories for use in sermons, the preacher asks the same kinds of questions that we have brought to the interpretation of Scripture throughout this practice. There are, however, essential and unmovable differences between the fixed text of Scripture and the stories we

---

27. Kolbet, *Augustine and the Cure of Souls*, 180.

narrate in our sermons; and such differences must shape how stories show up in our sermons. Let me briefly address two essential differences. First, though stories can be in a sense a continuation of and an interpretation of Scripture, they do not have the same authority and cannot replace the witness of the prophets and apostles. Scripture precedes our stories in every sense, including epistemologically. We do not use story to create a lens independent of Scripture through which to understand Scripture; rather, we interpret the story's events through the lens of Scripture. Scripture shows us what it means to be human, to be bound to others in families and cities, to be jealous, greedy, fearful, and so on. Second, as stated above, unlike the fixed text of Scripture that we have received, sermon stories are always our construction. If they are stories in which we are involved, we are author, narrator, and participant. If they are stories about others, we are at the least both author and narrator. Sermons in which personal stories take up a far larger portion of space and attention than Scripture are problematic. Our careful use of them must reflect the primacy of Scripture.

As I am baking my sermon throughout the rhythm of my week, often a story or vignette will pop into my head. It is a raw story in need of interpretation. I use stories sparingly and follow a two-step process to determine if a story is helpful, appropriate, or necessary for a sermon, or if it is simply a life raft for a sermon in trouble. First, examine the story theologically. Second, examine its relationship to the Scripture of the sermon.

Step 1: Examine the Story Theologically

The questions used to examine a story theologically are similar to the tools used for the five previous questions we have explored for the theological practice of proclamation.

What do I see? What is happening in the story? Determine which details are important and which are not. Be as concise as possible. In most cases in sermon stories, the rule "less is more" applies. Use contraction to tighten and shorten the story. Avoid imposing narrative flow.

Whom do *they* see? How do the actions of the participants in the story witness to *their* recognition of and response to Christ, if at all? Is this a "Lord, when did we see you?" or an "If you believe, you will see

God's glory" kind of story? Use this question for examination. Avoid
forcing a story into these categories.

Whom do I see? How does this story reveal the identity of Jesus
Christ to me, the preacher? What can I see that the participants in the
story cannot see? What can I see and name along with the participants
in the story? Here the preacher facilitates recognition.

What do *they* say of us? How do the actions of the participants in
the story witness to their recognition of our shared identity in Christ
in a disobedient world, if at all?

What does this story say of us? How does this story witness to our
identity as disciples and the church in this place?

Step 2: Examine the Story in Relationship to the Text

This second step asks the preacher to consider the relationship of
the story and the Scripture texts and the proportion of the two in a
sermon. Too often preachers walk out of Scripture into the world of
personal story and never return to Scripture. Frequently, they barely
stop in Scripture's room on their way. At the worst, they skip through
it with seemingly little curiosity and spend no time looking around it.
This tool reminds us not to substitute the more accessible world of
personal story for the textured world of Scripture. These questions are
not exhaustive. Each preacher knows her tendencies, shortcuts, and
predispositions in sermon construction. Here are sample questions to
hold us accountable to the privilege and task of preaching.

- How does the story point to Christ (through the actions of the
  participants) as revealed in the Scripture texts at the heart of the
  sermon?
- If the story has little to do with Christ, what is it about? If it does
  not function like a beam of light revealing Christ, how does it
  function?
- How much space (words, minutes) does the story take up? How
  much space (words, minutes) does the exploration of Scripture
  take up?
- Have I adequately attended to Scripture or left it too quickly and
  gone into story? Does my turn to story preclude me from digging

deeper or more fully into Scripture, reading around, reading it intratextually, and so on?

- In the story's placement in the sermon, do I return to Scripture and to Christ proclaimed there, or do I leave these behind?

The Differences between Stories, Symbols, and Examples

This sixth question helps the preacher use stories to witness to Jesus Christ. What about symbols and examples? Can they witness to Christ? It's a question worth asking for at least two reasons. Symbols and examples show up in our sermons, and it's the preacher's job to know what they are doing while they are there. Distinguishing the limits and uses of each of these rhetoric forms will clarify the role of stories in sermons.

Like Scripture itself, stories can witness to Christ because of their narrative density. As described in chapter 1, a witness testifies to something that has happened. The role of the preacher as witness is to testify to Jesus Christ—not something else. Ricoeur says, "The witness does not testify about isolated and contingent fact but about the radical, global meaning of human experience. It is Yahweh himself who is witnessed to in the testimony."[28] Can symbols and examples also do this?

Symbols can be a shorthand way to point to a story, a narrated event. The symbol of the cross is an authoritative summary of Christ's death and resurrection. Likewise, the abbreviation "9/11" is an authoritative summary of a set of events that changed the world on September 11, 2001. They have narrative density, assuming that those listening know the longhand version of what they symbolize. But other symbols lack the kernel of narrated events necessary to be able to witness to something that happened. The symbol of a snowdrop, as it pushes through the late winter snow, lacks the historic density needed to witness to the resurrected Christ. This symbol might please the imagination, but it does not witness to Christ, whose identity is given in his incarnated life, death, resurrection, and ascension.

What about examples?[29] Like testimony, examples are about something that has happened. Usually they have the character of narrative

28. Ricoeur, "Hermeneutics of Testimony," 131.
29. What follows is taken from Paul Ricoeur, "Hermeneutics of Testimony."

density. The question to ask of our sermon examples is, "Examples of what?" We often use examples to depict the behaviors that are a norm for Christians. This is an example of what discipleship looks like. Or humility. The challenge is that examples point to a norm or form of life, rather than to Christ, whose own life has shaped this form of life for the Christian community. If I give a concrete example of what it looks like to work for justice through solidarity with the poor in the church's neighborhood, the example most likely points to the practice of solidarity, but not to the one to whom solidarity with the poor is a response. Examples cast a beam of light from the example to the norm or exemplary form of life. Listeners might be more aware of this form of life and its norm for Christians. But this is not testimony; it does not witness to Jesus Christ.

The preacher will use all these forms.[30] Pleasing the imagination through symbols and images and providing examples of the forms and practices of the Christian life belong in sermons. But so does our witness to Jesus Christ. We often have too little to say about him. Too easily and too often Christ drops out of our sermons. The beam of light in sermons can point here and there and everywhere. All Six Questions of the Sermon try to ensure this doesn't happen.

A chapter discussing the uses and limits of personal stories in sermons could be misinterpreted as a discussion about the uses and limits of the preacher's relationship to the personal stories of her parishioners. This would be a grave mistake. The people entrusted to us by God, as Paul says, are our joy and crown (Phil. 4:1; 1 Thess. 2:19). We carry them with us as we go about our days and wake in the night (Prov. 3:3). We carry both their stories and their storyless places. The pastor, as she binds herself to both God's people and God's Word, has the great privilege of seeing with her own eyes the redemption of both in Christ's embrace of creaturely difference.

In an interview in which Pope Francis describes his "method" of preparing a homily, he suggests love as a criterion for preaching. He includes two essential elements:

> Listen to the lives of people. If you do not listen to people, how can you preach? The closer you are to people, the better you will preach or bring the

---

30. Buttrick's *Homiletic: Moves and Structures*, 127–54, presents a helpful section on the concise use of stories and examples in sermons.

word of God nearer their lives. In this way, you link the word of God to a human experience that has need of this word. . . . The more distant you are from people and their problems, the more you will take refuge in a theology that is framed as "You must," and "You must not," which communicates nothing, which is empty, abstract, lost in nothing, in thoughts. At such times we respond with our words to questions that nobody is asking. . . .

To preach to people it is necessary to look at them, to know how to look and how to listen, to enter into the ebb and flow of their lives, to immerse oneself in them . . . [or] in silence look into their eyes.[31]

Our people, whom we are bound to in love, are the reason we care about our sermons. They deserve the best of what we have to offer. They do not need to listen to us. They are not obligated to show up and put themselves in a position to be addressed by our humble words. They come ready to listen, I believe. Our sermons are acts of love because, as Pope Francis says, people have need of God's Word, not to fix their problems or tell them what to do but as a reminder that the living God speaks to, addresses, and calls to them and us and, through the Holy Spirit, gives us the ears to hear his word. God is not an idea, a proposition, a doctrine, an abstract principle, or a universal experience. Jesus Christ, son of the God of Israel, is alive and way out in front of any of us.

Thus our sermon preparation is an act of love, in a sense, no different or less important than listening to the lives of parishioners, attentively and reverently, especially when it is difficult. Jesus Christ, alive, speaks and calls to us where we are, not where we are not. And where we are, as creatures, is in a world of stubborn particularity, of material realities and inequalities, which are the hallmark of creaturely existence. None of us is an everywoman or everyman. Yet Jesus Christ speaks and calls to us through his embrace and redemption of our creaturely existence. Greater love there is not. To try to listen to him with our people, to practice the corporate posture of putting ourselves in a position to be addressed by him, is indeed a deep act of love—for our parishioners, for the church, and for the world for which Christ died. The Six Questions are offered as one way we might learn to listen together and have some sense of what to do in a sermon with what we hear.

31. Gerard O'Connell, "Francis the Preacher," *America Magazine*, December 5–12, 2016, 24.

7

Using the Six Questions

Sermon Form and Sermon Examples

Introduction: The Six Questions and Sermon Forms

Every country and region has its own cuisine. Each is built on a handful of basic ingredients found and grown locally. Mexican cuisine is corn, beans, and chili peppers. Thai cuisine is curry paste, lemongrass, coconut milk, and rice. Go to South India and it's dried beans, cardamom, cinnamon, garam masala. Head to France and you find bread, butter, cheese, fresh herbs, sea salt, and so on. The particularities of a region's native habitat determine what can grow there: altitude, temperature, rainfall, soil acidity, and moisture content, to name a few. Lemongrass grows in the tropical grasslands of Indonesia. Chili peppers flourish in the dry desert soil of their native Mexico. The French understand this well. They developed the idea of *terroir*, from *la terre*, the French word for the land. Terroir refers to all the environmental factors that form a specific habitat. A terroir can be the side of a hill in a vineyard or a single row of vines. A good vintner knows this and works with it. A bottle's distinctive taste is an expression of the terroir in the wine.

The Six Questions of the Sermon serve as basic ingredients in sermon preparation, which, like lemongrass and butter, spring from

their natural habitat. This book has argued that the church is the soil
in which text and people are rooted, the natural habitat for interpreting Scripture for proclamation. The theological movement of the Six
Questions tries to work with the sermon's terroir, the single Word of
God in the Spirit's hands, heard and lived in the specific contexts of
its congregations and people.

The questions begin with attentiveness to the Scripture and its center and completion, Jesus Christ. From there they take the preacher to
Christ's personal and corporate address, to recognition of the identity
given to the church, and finally to the recognition of how the people of
God inhabit this identity for and in a disobedient world. The movement
from attentiveness to hearing to recognition will, we hope, participate
in the Spirit's formation of an acceptable people in God's sight. We
hope our sermons will not be empty words. Like the rain and snow,
which water the earth and bring forth seed (Isa. 55:10–11), Sunday by
Sunday preachers hope their sermons will accomplish the purposes
for which God intends them. They hope their sermons will help to
form a people whose common life is the primary form of interpreting
Scripture, a people who are a witness to the nations of Jesus Christ,
Son of the God of Israel and their creator. Just as the Word spoken
takes flesh in the incarnate Jesus, so the words of Scripture must take
flesh in the church.

To think of the Six Questions as basic ingredients also helps us
understand how to use them in the weekly round of sermon preparation. They are the staples on our kitchen shelves, from which a rich
variety of sermons can be prepared. Burritos this Sunday, stuffed po-
blanos next Sunday. They are not a checklist or a regimented method.
Proportions differ meal by meal, week by week. Using the Six Questions
in sermon preparation does not mean that the preacher's responses
to each will appear in every sermon. Because preaching is quotidian,
preachers can mix it up. Skip the garam masala so the cardamom is
more prominent. The occasion, the specific texts of Scripture, and the
people gathered to listen with the preacher will all shape this weekly
feasting on the Word. Yet this is not a license to cast aside or summarily
dismiss any of the questions. In the busy round of parish life, it is too
easy to turn Scripture into something we manage in order to do our
jobs, to skip the hard work of listening, or to run around so we rarely

put ourselves in a position to be addressed by the living Christ. The hope is that these questions are easy enough to be remembered and straightforward enough to be used—so we might linger a little longer in Scripture's room and have some idea of what to do there.

Form and Content

Form and content are not two separate entities in sermons. Thomas Long emphasizes this point when he defines sermon form as the *"form of the content."*[1] I have expanded his definition in order to emphasize the theological movement of the Six Questions. Sermon form is *the form of the movement of the content*, as preacher and congregation try to put themselves in a position to be addressed by God's Word.

The quotidian nature of the practice of preaching, as well as the connection between form and content, shapes how we approach the form of our sermons. They don't all need to be the same. They should not be. Sermon forms are not neutral. They are not simply containers or boxes for their content.[2] A sermon form is a part of its meaning. For example, if I always shape my sermon by beginning with a problem in the world and then move to how Scripture addresses this problem (what is loosely called the problem-resolution form), I most likely have created a sermon that is easy to listen to and follow.[3] But if I use it exclusively and I get used to listening to Scripture with my congregation through this single form, then I also communicate things I might not mean to about God, God's Word, and God's world. First, does God's Word solve our problems on our terms? Not very often. It calls, judges, and disrupts. As said in chapter 2, our sermons are one place we may be called to subordinate or even reject values that contradict Jesus's. The problem-resolution form is not designed to do this. Second, God's Word is not a response to the world (problems or otherwise) that precedes and exists independently of it. Theologically speaking,

1. Thomas Long, *The Witness of Preaching*, 3rd ed. (Louisville: Westminster John Knox, 2016), 137 (emphasis original).

2. For a fuller discussion of sermon forms and examples of specific sermon forms see Long, *Witness of Preaching*, chaps. 4–8, pp. 113–253.

3. See discussion about the problem-resolution form in Long, *Witness of Preaching*, 148–52.

Scripture precedes our problems and provides the lens through which to understand and respond to them. As discussed in chapter 4, we do not begin with an understanding of our social contexts that is derived independently from Scripture. We turn to what Scripture teaches us about such differences through its own texts. The problem-resolution form, if used too often, obscures this commitment.

Our guide to a rich variety of faithful sermon forms is Scripture itself. Various forms and genres are used to communicate the gospel over time to a wide variety of peoples and cultures. All of Scripture's diverse literary forms are put in service of the communication of the gospel. No one genre or form is adequate for the communication of God's Word. Inductive and deductive sermons can work, as well as a combination of the two.

The preacher arranges her sermon in a manner that will communicate the shared listening to God's Word. Augustine proves helpful in clarifying the relationship between the interpretation of Scripture and its communication in sermons. Augustine divided his preaching manual, *On Christian Teaching*, into two parts, based on the two aspects of sermon preparation: "the process of discovering what we need to learn, and the process of presenting what we have learnt."[4] Only in the fourth book does he turn to the question of how the preacher communicates Scripture in the written and spoken words of the sermon. Augustine, a classically trained rhetorician, provides this pragmatic guideline for sermon form. "The best method is one by which the listener hears the truth and understands what he hears."[5] Rhetorical forms, literary devices, and persuasive language all improve the sermon's clarity, while sermon form and the delights of language serve the lucidity of the sermon.

Thanks to the New Homiletic, the preacher has a well-stocked cupboard of sermon forms, none of which need be dismissed out of hand. The New Homiletic was born out of a strong critique of the limitations of the deductive form of the sermon. The deductive form moves from the general (usually a proposition) to the specific. The sermon begins with the theme, proposition, thesis, or principle of the sermon and

4. Augustine, *On Christian Teaching* 1.1.
5. Augustine, *On Christian Teaching* 4.71.

then moves into persuasive argument, illustration, and application of the main point. This general pattern, which has had a lasting influence on North American preaching, was passed down through two historical approaches to preaching.

The Franciscans and Dominicans developed the "university sermon" in the late medieval period. This approach begins with a central proposition or point and breaks it down into three subsections.[6] We know it as the "three points and a poem" approach to preaching. The "Puritan Plain Style" was developed in England and New England in the late sixteenth century. Like the university sermon, it had three sections: exposition of Scripture, doctrine, and application. The exposition and reflection on Scripture lead to general principles to be applied at the end of the sermon.

The New Homiletic's quest for an alternative to deductive preaching opened the door to the rich variety of sermon forms that appear in North American pulpits today.[7] The New Homiletic's proponents questioned the wisdom of conforming every sermon to a single form based on logical argument. Influenced by the New Hermeneutic and literary and language studies, the question of the relationship between the sermon form and the literary form of Scripture became central. Sermon form, they concluded, was an expression of the literary form of Scripture; to craft a sermon around the literary form of the text allowed the listener to encounter and experience the Word. Forms of inductive preaching that move from the specific to the general became the dominant sermon form: storytelling and narrative preaching in a variety of fashions.

The inductive sermon that moves from the specific to the general is well suited to the theological movement of the Six Questions of the Sermon. It can help to keep the preacher and congregation rooted in the text, narrative and nonnarrative portions alike. It can invite inquiry. But Scripture needs interpretation. The preacher is called to be more than a storyteller. She is witness, confessor, and theologian.

6. O. Wesley Allen provides a concise overview of the history of sermonic form in the introduction to *The Renewed Homiletic* (Minneapolis: Fortress, 2010), 1–18. I am indebted to his concise introduction for my remarks here.

7. For an overview with examples of the main sermon forms of the New Homiletic, see Richard Eslinger, *A New Hearing: Living Options in Homiletic Method* (Nashville: Abingdon, 1987); O. Allen, *Renewed Homiletic*.

Propositions, doctrine, arguments, and clear statements find a rightful place in sermons. The following sermon examples model this. Like any artisan, the preacher needs knowledge of the tools of her craft, and she must be able to distinguish various sermon forms, know their uses and limits, and like a good cook, experiment with them.

The proportions of Augustine's preaching manual help to put questions of sermon form into perspective: three books on how to interpret Scripture, one on how to communicate it. This great rhetorician knew that not all preachers were master craftspeople of the spoken or written word. While Augustine preferred wisdom served with a side dish of eloquence, he knew the lack of it was not an impediment to proclaiming God's Word.[8] In Christ's incarnation God has made the most transient of all things—frail human words and frail human flesh—the instruments of divine wisdom. No amount of eloquence or artistry, no amount of cleverness or adeptness at using the latest sermon techniques can substitute for a life bound to Scripture and to God's people in the church for the sake of the world. "What use is a golden key, if it cannot unlock what we want unlocked, and what is wrong with a wooden one, if it can?"[9] If preachers are called to care deeply about form in their sermons, it is the form of their own lives, with and among the people of God, the form that preaches and witnesses day by day, with or without our words. For as Augustine declares to his congregation, "What after all am I, but someone needing to be set free with you, cured with you?"[10] In Christ we have been set free. God has given us ears to hear him and through his Holy Spirit has made us into a people able to respond.

In the three sermon examples that follow, I provide a word about the context in which the sermons were preached and a summary of my preparation using the Six Questions of the Sermon.

8. "Learning has a lot in common with eating: to cater for the dislikes of the majority even the nutrients essential to life must be made appetizing." Augustine, *On Christian Teaching* 4.10.

9. Augustine, *On Christian Teaching* 4.10.

10. Augustine, *Sermons (1–19) on the Old Testament,* part 3, vol. 8 of *The Works of St. Augustine: A Translation for the Twenty-First Century,* trans. Edmund Hill, ed. John E. Rotelle (Hyde Park, NY: New City, 1990), 9.10.

First Sermon Example: Psalm 19[11]

A word about context: I preached this at Wycliffe college's weekly community Eucharist. The form and movement of the psalm through its three sections shapes the movement of the content of the sermon. I focus on hearing each section in relation to the others. Christ does not explicitly come into the psalm or the sermon until the final section.

Question 1: What Do I See? The Preacher as Witness

▶ **Main action:** Attentively read the appointed Scriptures.

Psalm 19 is divided into three sections: the created order (vv. 1–6), the law (vv. 7–9), and the psalmist's response (vv. 10–14). The language of verses 1–6 is eloquent and metaphorical. The description of the day and night telling their tale to the ends of the earth echoes Jesus's words that the created order will do the same about him. "I tell you, if these were silent, the stones would shout out" (Luke 19:40). The description of the law in verses 7–9 is a catalog of its benefits. The description of the sun coming out of its pavilion like a bridegroom and champion (vv. 5–6) echoes descriptions of Jesus as the bridegroom, the true light, the morning star, and the sun of righteousness (Isa. 61:10; Mal. 4:2; Luke 5:33–35; Rev. 2:28). This psalm is a kind of retelling of the creation story, making explicit the connection between God's creation of the natural world and God's commandments for the human flourishing within it.

Question 2: Whom Do I See? The Preacher as Witness to Christ

▶ **Main action:** Describe the identity of Jesus Christ revealed in the text.

God creates both the natural world and the law and commandments with the single purpose of glorifying their creator. I see a God who has provided for his creation ("then shall I be whole and sound," v. 13) through both the abundance of the earth and the law and commandments. In the psalmist's prayer (v. 13), I see a God who has created us to take our place in his creation as servants. I see Jesus, who was

---

11. I am using the version of Psalm 19 that appears in the Canadian *Book of Alternative Services*, which is taken from the US *Book of Common Prayer*.

present at the foundation of creation, coming out of his pavilion like a bridegroom, like the sun of righteousness (John 1:2; Col. 1:15–17).

Question 3: What Is Christ's Word to Me? The Preacher as Confessor

▶ **Main action:** Hear God's address to you and receive God's mercy and judgment.

This psalm fills me with a desire to more deeply love and follow the precepts of God. I am stirred by its language and respond in my heart,

> "O God, you are my God, I seek you,
>   my soul thirsts for you;
> my flesh faints for you,
>   as in a dry and weary land where there is no water."
>   Psalm 63:1

Practically speaking, I don't know what this means. Should I be praying more, reading Scripture more? Changing my life, selling all that I have and giving it to the poor? Working for climate change? My response is also to ask myself, What are my presumptuous sins (Ps. 19:13), especially as a North American? I feel despair and a sense of urgency over climate change. But what do I do with this?

Question 4: What Is Christ's Word to Us? The Preacher as Theologian

▶ **Main action:** Hear God's address to the church and one's own congregation in its particular context.

I hear God saying, I have created you to be whole and sound and have given you everything you need to become this. You won't become whole and sound on your own but bound to my law, commandments, and Word, bound to my Son and, in him, bound to your neighbor and the created order. Look to Jesus to see what it means to be whole and sound.

Question 5: What Is Christ's Word about Us? The Preacher as Theologian of a Broken Body

▶ **Main action:** Describe the identity of the church and the disciple given in Christ's word and address to us.

We are creatures and servants (v. 13). We have been created as part of a complex, interconnected whole that reflects its creator, the God of Israel and the father of Jesus Christ. God has not left us on our own to wander through this world or use it as a playground for our misplaced desires. We have been created with a place, identity, and purpose. Baptism into the body of Jesus Christ, through God's gift of water, is a sign that we are not the creator or author of our lives.

Question 6: What Does It Look Like? The Preacher as Witness to Christ in a Disobedient World

▶ **Main action:** Facilitate recognition of how the identity of Christ is inhabited in a broken and disobedient world.

The psalmist says that our identity as creatures in this interconnected world will often mean repenting (v. 12–13). This feels right to me. My response to the majesty of this psalm is to say, "Who am I that you are mindful of me?" (8:4). A recall a story that demonstrates this principle. Each year the Russian, Greek, and other Orthodox churches bless the waters, rivers, and lakes in the liturgy known as the Great Blessing of the Waters. It takes place on January 5 and 6, around the feast of Christ's baptism and theophany in the Jordan. This past year in Bristol Bay, Alaska, the Russian Orthodox bishop Benjamin Peterson combined this liturgy with a message of concern from the church over the potential development of the Pebble Mine, which threatens the waters in the bay.

SERMON ON PSALM 19

Whenever my family hikes, as we do often in the American West, I end the day with my pockets and backpack filled with rocks. I love rocks. They become paperweights, page holders, bookends, soap dishes, and part of my garden wall. My family is amused by my habit, and my children indulge me by presenting me with a small rock from the top of each mountain they summit. Why do I love rocks? I love them because each tells a story, often millions of years old, in its layers, the form of its grain, and so on. It's like the Bible, I tell my children. Like rocks, the Bible tells a story, and like rocks, most people don't know how to read it. It's strange that I make this comparison because I'm not good at reading rocks, keeping straight the differences between sedimentary, igneous, and metamorphic. Last summer our son gave me a book to help with this and to deepen my knowledge of what I already love. It's called *Reading the Rocks: The Autobiography of the Earth*. In it the author, geologist Marcia Bjornerud, says that the different kinds of rocks are like different literary genres, and she writes to include her readers in the four-billion-year-old conversation between rocks, water, and all forms of life.

In a sense that's precisely what our psalmist is doing in Psalm 19: showing us how to read God's handiwork, not just rocks, but the four-billion-year-old conversation between rocks, water, all forms of life, and their creator.

The psalmist tells us this:

> "The heavens declare the glory of God,
> and the firmament shows his handiwork.
> One day tells its tale to another,
> and one night imparts its knowledge to another.
>
> Although they have no words or language,
> and their voices are not heard,
> Their sound has gone out into all lands,
> and their message to the ends of the world."
>
>   Psalm 19:1–4

What is the sermon or message they preach with their intricate and interconnected beauty? What tale does one day pass on to the next? It is this: God made all this marvel to declare his glory. The heavens with their stars flung wide, and all creation.

And we probably agree, even as we live among asphalt and cement. The state of the created world, its fragility and our place in it, has taken center stage in our national conversations in a way it has not in past generations. We are now discussing the land, where our food comes from, global warming and rising seas, and what is happening to coral reefs and animal habitats. As young people come of age and think about their futures and this planet's future, they are listening closely to the tale the day tells the night, listening and responding by what they study in school, the jobs they look for, what they eat, and so on. We need to pay attention to them.

But look where the psalmist's reading of the created order leads him. After praising creation for the first six verses, in verses 7 and 8 his praise seems to take a different direction.

> "The law of the Lord is perfect
>   and revives the soul; . . .
>
> The statutes of the Lord are just
>   and rejoice the heart;
> the commandment of the Lord is clear
>   and gives light to the eyes."
>   Psalm 19:7–8

Is this a different direction? Here, the psalmist catalogs the Torah, or law, the way Marcia Bjornerud catalogs the mineral composition of sedimentary rock. In verses 7–9 the psalmist identifies six aspects of the Torah: law, testimony, precepts, commandment, fear, and judgment. He then describes seven characteristics of these six aspects: the Torah is perfect, sure, just, clear, clean, true, and righteous. After such careful study, what is his conclusion? The law is to be desired more than fine gold; it is sweeter, far sweeter than honey from the comb (v. 10). It is a pearl of great price, a treasure hidden in a field.

Would we make the same connection that the psalmist does between the created world and the law God gave to Israel? Would we go so far as to conclude that the same God who made this world, which sustains us, also made the commandments to sustain us *in it*? Just as God created the moon and the tides to be bound to one another and the sun and the planets to stay within the boundaries of their established rhythm, so too God has created his commandments, which establish the rhythms of our complex and interconnected life together with God and one another, with rocks, water, and all forms of life—and their creator.

This is exactly what the psalmist declares. Just as God created the planets in their courses to give him glory, so too God gives us a rhythm to live by. And because God is creator of both, God makes us a promise. In living by the rhythms of God's law we, like the stars, are made a thing of beauty that declares God's glory. Imagine: our common life a thing of beauty to rival the stars. Our ordinary life with one another, day in and day out, a thing of beauty. Imagine if the young people today who are working on organic farms and trying to protect the wilderness knew that such a promise—and way of life—was ours. And theirs.

Psalm 19 is a classic affirmation that God's gift of the law is *essentially bound up with* God's gift of the created world, of the universe itself. The psalmist praises this: "The commandment of the Lord is clear / and gives light to the eyes" (v. 8). But his knowledge of God's gifts of creation and the law do not end with words of praise. In verses 11–13 the psalmist moves beyond praise to self-examination and repentance: "Above all, keep your servant from presumptuous sins; / let them not get dominion over me; / then shall I be whole and sound" (v. 13). Is this a direction we would go in?

Throughout Scripture, not only in Psalm 19, this affirmation (that the God who created the world has also given us a way to live in it) leads to a response of self-examination and repentance. Again, I ask, would we follow the psalmist here? Does seeing and knowing that God has given us *both* the created world and his commandments for human flourishing lead us to self-examination and repentance?

Scripture calls us to repentance. Our repentance, like the psalmist's, witnesses to our understanding that God created both the world and the law as gifts to his people for their flourishing. Notice that on these very terms God criticizes Judah for its faithlessness, for severing the connection between the gift of the created world and the gift of the law, and for their failure to repent.

> Declare this in the house of Jacob,
> proclaim it in Judah:
> Hear this, O foolish and senseless people,
> who have eyes, but do not see,
> who have ears, but do not hear.
> Do you not fear me? says the LORD;
> Do you not tremble before me?
> I placed the sand as a boundary for the sea,
> a perpetual barrier that it cannot pass;
> though the waves toss, they cannot prevail,
> though they roar, they cannot pass over it.
> But this people has a stubborn and rebellious heart;
> they have turned aside and gone away.
> They do not say in their hearts,
> "Let us fear the LORD our God,

> who gives the rain in its season,
>   the autumn rain and the spring rain,
> and keeps for us
>   the weeks appointed for the harvest."
>   Jeremiah 5:20–24

This weekend was the five-year anniversary of the 2011 tsunami in Japan, so we know the chaos and destruction that happens when the sea violates the barrier God established for it. Once in a long while, the waves toss and prevail, and we cry out because of the damage, destruction, and senseless loss of life. But far more damage, destruction, and senseless loss of life arises not from the sea crossing the boundaries God established, but from our crossing the boundaries God has established for our lives with him and one another. This can be seen in all the ways we refuse to be bound to our neighbor: coveting, killing, committing adultery, stealing, giving false witness, and making idols of wealth, power and influence, and so on. In any calendar year far more destruction arises from greed alone, which blinds us to our neighbor, than from floods or natural disasters.

Imagine if the moon said to the tide, "I refuse to be bound to you." Or if the sun declared that no one could rotate around it anymore. Imagine if fall refused to follow summer and if spring refused to deal with winter's frozen earth. Does our insistence that we can do our own thing make any more sense? Paul asks if the eye can say to the hand, "I have no need of you" (1 Cor. 12:21). Can the elbow similarly tell the shoulder, "I claim my right to be independent of you"?

No, I don't think so. I would guess that young people who are turning to the land and trying to find a way to live in a sustainable fashion are looking for such a connection—between the land and life-giving rhythms of our dependence on it and one another. We have good news to tell them. It is the same good news that one day tells to another. God did not create his creatures for lives of disconnection from the land, from the rhythms of day and night, or from one another—and certainly not from him. God, the creator of this marvelous world, my body, and my life, has given us a path to follow in the way that we *live within this world*. God has created us to be a thing of beauty, created us along with the stars to declare God's glory. We have good news to tell indeed.

To this end Jesus steps out of the pavilion God set for the Son in the uttermost edge of the heavens (v. 6). The psalmist tells us that Jesus steps forth like a bridegroom from his marriage chamber, like a champion to run his course (v. 5). But instead of running like a champion, God sends Jesus as a servant. Jesus gives up his equality with God and takes the form of a servant.

Why? Despite sin's determination to have dominion over us and our determination to push God aside, God can no more cast us aside than cast aside the stars and moon. It turns out that just as God's gift of the law is *bound up with* God's gift of the created world, so too is his love. God declares to Israel and to us, "If any of you could break my covenant with the day and my covenant with the night, so that day and night would not come at their appointed time, *only then* could my covenant with my servant David be broken" (Jer. 33:20–21).

Can we break God's covenant with the night (even you who email me at 3 a.m.)? No. Can we make it so that the day does not follow the night? No (a reminder that this warming planet is in God's hands as well as ours). Thus can we break God's covenant with us? No. God sends his Son to dwell among the earthly creation—to walk with us, live with us, and ultimately to be a sinless savior. Why? Because in his Son, crucified and risen, God sets his world right. In Christ, God frees us from the grip of sin and death so that in him we can take our place with all creation—young and old, day and night—to declare his glory.

Spring is coming. The night skies are clear. Go outside tonight. Look up at the stars. And read the rocks God has made: they tell the story of our life together.

Amen.

Second Sermon Example: John 3:13–17 and 1 Corinthians 1:1–24

A word about context: I preached this in the Wycliffe seminary chapel at the beginning of a new academic year, in the service in which we were celebrating Holy Cross Day. The congregation included students, faculty, and staff across denominations and degree programs. The tone is formal, appropriate for the start of an academic year and for establishing my role as chaplain.

Question 1: *What Do I See? The Preacher as Witness*

▶ **Main action:** Attentively read the appointed Scriptures.

In the John text, the sending of Jesus into the world immediately caught my attention (3:17). The shape of God's love is the sending of Jesus. I moved to other passages about sending as the form of God's love (Matt. 9:35–38; John 17:18–19; 20:21). We participate in this love as Jesus sends us.

In the 1 Corinthians text, Paul describes his ministry in the midst of a divided church. I focused on Paul's phrase "so that the cross of Christ might not be emptied of its power" (1:17). Paul says this in the context of division within the Corinthian church. His phrase implies that, through his ministry, the cross *could* be emptied of its power. The "measure" of his ministry is that the cross not be emptied of its power.

Here Paul gives us a definition of ministry in a divided church and world. His definition both binds us to Jesus and makes us stewards of the power of Christ's cross. This leads me to define ministry in these terms: "Think of us in this way, as servants of Christ and stewards of God's mysteries" (1 Cor. 4:1).

Question 2: *Whom Do I See? The Preacher as Witness to Christ*

▶ **Main action:** Describe the identity of Jesus Christ revealed
in the text.

I see Christ, in whom the Father's love (i.e., his sending of Christ), Christ's cross and its power, and our being sent are all inseparable. Christ binds us to himself and to his ministry through the cross. This is the power we participate in. He has joined himself to us from start to finish—God's love and sending, Christ's cross and its purpose are one in him. I see Christ, who will draw all things to himself (Eph. 1:9–10).

Question 3: *What Is Christ's Word to Me? The Preacher as Confessor*

▶ **Main action:** Hear God's address to you and receive God's mercy
and judgment.

I hear this as a word of judgment, which leads to self-examination. How foolish am I really? Do I rely on eloquence and reason and goodwill? How naive am I about the depth of division in the church and the world? Do I really believe what Paul says about the power of the cross?

Question 4: What Is Christ's Word to Us? The Preacher as Theologian

▶ **Main action:** Hear God's address to the church and one's own congregation in its particular context.

Because my congregation is the seminary community, I hear a word to us about our vocation. That word is both encouragement and warning. The power of the cross is the salvation of the world's divisions. We can easily empty it of its power.

I hear an implicit description of how intractable is the nature of the world's sin.

Question 5: What Is Christ's Word about Us? The Preacher as Theologian of a Broken Body

▶ **Main action:** Describe the identity of the church and the disciple given in Christ's word and address to us.

We are fools like everyone else, fools whom God, in his love for us and the world, has made stewards of the very power of the world's salvation, the cross. We "measure" our ministry by whether the cross has been emptied of its power. As stewards, it is not ours, but we participate in God's sending of Jesus as we are sent.

Question 6: What Does It Look Like? The Preacher as Witness to Christ in a Disobedient World

▶ **Main action:** Facilitate recognition of how the identity of Christ is inhabited in a broken and disobedient world.

Our identity in Christ is lived in our preaching the gospel of Christ crucified to all to whom he was sent (1 Cor. 1:17, 21–22). I use the story of André Trocmé because he is doing explicitly that—I tell about getting pushback. (Trocmé was a French Protestant pastor who, during World War II, helped to save the lives of Jews and other refugees. He received criticism at the end of the war for protecting and pastoring

German prisoners of war.) It's a long story, made even longer because I first need to introduce him. I place it at the beginning to try to balance its narrative weight, so it is not the only thing listeners remember. It also functions to establish my presence, tone, and authority in the pulpit, to let the congregation settle into listening. (Because this sermon was preached at the beginning of a new academic year, it was the first time new students heard me preach at the seminary.) I interpret the story of Trocmé in the course of the sermon. I also return to the question of what our Christian identity looks like explicitly in nonnarrative description.

SERMON ON JOHN 3:13–17 AND 1 CORINTHIANS 1:1–24

Between the years of 1939 and 1944, the people of a remote mountain region in central France quietly hid between one and five thousand refugees. Many were Jewish children. The village was Le Chambon. Students in my classes have read about it. The people of this isolated plateau were farmers and teachers. They ran boarding houses and cafés. Through a secret network of aid organizations, they hid refugees on their farms and in their barns, in their schools and boarding houses; and using an underground railroad, they led many through the region's dense woods over the border into Switzerland.

These remarkable actions happened through their local Protestant church and the leadership of their pastor, André Trocmé, as well as his wife, Magda, and copastor, Edouard Theis. This small, remote village church, with the help of an international network, was the kind of church we all dream our own could be. They saved lives, many lives, at the risk of their own in the name of Jesus Christ. For that work, the Yad Vashem of Israel conferred the title of "Righteous Among the Nations"—the highest gentile honor in Israel—on the Trocmés, Theis, and, in time, over forty others. In 1990, in a highly unusual act, the title "Righteous Among the Nations" was conferred on the entire village of Le Chambon.

But that isn't the story I want to tell about this French pastor and his congregation at the beginning of this sermon in the first week of the school year, on a Wednesday known as Holy Cross Day, when we lift high Christ's cross. Rather, it's a story of how Trocmé carried out his ministry at the end of the war. After Germany had been defeated by the

Allies, there were about 120 German soldiers being held as prisoners on the outskirts of Le Chambon. It was August 1945. Pastor Trocmé said, "Because the prisoners were in my parish, I automatically became their chaplain."[12] His focus (and that of his church) turned from protecting Jews and other refugees to protecting German prisoners of war. Many in the area, including resistance fighters, wanted them executed. Trocmé would have none of it. He did what churches do: he led services for the German soldiers; he preached. He pastored and taught. He wrote a catechism of sorts, starting with the Ten Commandments and ending with justice, truth, and nonviolence. These are virtues, Trocmé told the German prisoners, "we can always practice because God has forgiven our sins through the resurrection of Jesus Christ."[13]

Each Sunday Trocmé delivered the same sermon to his two congregations. In the morning he preached his sermon in French in his parish church, and in the afternoon he preached it in German at the prison camp. Neither group was happy about it. The French accused him of being a spy for the Germans, and the Germans accused him of being a spy for the French. His response? "I was just trying to preach the gospel." Trocmé refused to see either the French or the Germans as unilaterally guilty or innocent. He refused to see either group solely through the lens of friend or foe, victim or victor—but rather through Christ's eyes, all of them as Christ's lost children. So he proclaimed the single gospel of Christ's forgiveness to both.[14] Perhaps he had in mind the middle of Acts 11. When some of the apostles heard about Peter's experience in Joppa, they were silenced. And they praised God, saying, "Then God has given even to the Gentiles the repentance that leads to life" (v. 18).

How is difference to be addressed in Christ? In 1944 differences between the French and the Germans, differences in Paul's congregation in Corinth, and in 2016 differences within congregations, between denominations, and among neighbors? How?

I speak of all this, this afternoon, because our Scripture readings lead us to ask this question. Wycliffe is a Christian seminary whose vocation is to form students to be sent into the world to participate in Christ's ministry

12. Pierre Boismorand, ed., *Magda and André Trocmé: Resistance Figures*, trans. Jo-Anne Elder (Montreal: McGill-Queen's University Press, 2014), 143.
13. Boismorand, *Magda and André Trocmé*, 145.
14. This story is recounted in Boismorand, *Magda and André Trocmé*, 141–47.

through the church. This is the world into which God sent his Son. God so loved the world that he—what? We hear again this afternoon: "That he gave his only Son" (John 3:16). Differences among peoples in this world that God so loves are assumed and embraced in Christ's incarnation in our creaturely flesh. The question of how to address these differences is also created by Christ himself when he tells us, "As the Father has sent me, so I send you" (20:21). Send where? Not into some like-minded bubble. We are sent to the nations, to strangers, to enemies, to immigrants and migrants, to gay and homophobic people, to the police and young black men, to different political parties—and on and on—into the whole stew of differences that cause us to construct the divisive walls that Christ broke down.

It is the will and plan of God that we are sent. And more so—Jesus tells us *we are to pray* that we land in just this place. "The harvest is plentiful but the laborers are few," Jesus says. "Ask the Lord of the harvest to send out laborers into his harvest" (Matt. 9:37–38; Luke 10:2). Pray, Jesus tells us, that you land in just this difficult place.

This is Holy Cross Day, September 14—the day our Scripture readings and many churches put particular focus on the cross of Christ. The cross of Christ creates the single light by which we are to understand and participate in creaturely differences. The cross of Jesus Christ is the single shape of divine loving, embracing, suffering, and redeeming of the creaturely difference of his lost children. The death and resurrection of Jesus is the single power through which all peoples, near and far, are made one. That is what Paul reminds us of today as he responds to his own church struggling with differences. It is good news we need to hear again and again.

As you know, Paul begins the first of his two letters to the church in Corinth by naming the divisions that he has heard about from a distance. Chloe's people have reported to him that there are quarrels among the sisters and brothers there. Some say "I belong to Paul," or "I belong to Apollos," or "I belong to Cephas," or "I belong to Christ." Identity politics was alive and well before our time. Paul will have none of it. He writes to them, "Has Christ been divided? Was Paul crucified for you? Or were you baptized in the name of Paul? I thank God that I baptized none of you except Crispus and Gaius, so that no one can say that you were baptized in my name" (1 Cor. 1:13–15). And listen to what Paul says next in response to these divisions. Listen to what he identifies as the vocation of the church. "For Christ did not send me to baptize but to proclaim the gospel, and not with eloquent wisdom, *so that the cross of Christ might not be emptied of its power*" (1:17). So that the cross of Christ might not be emptied of its power.

We are shaped by and stand in the midst of the world's troubling and often violent complexities. This is both the glory and the sunk costs of being creatures. The vocation of the church Christ sends is to live, preach, and witness so that his cross is not emptied of its power. And how do we do that? First, we refuse to see such differences in the glare of the many false lights that illuminate them. We don't reduce differences to a struggle for power. We don't pretend they aren't there. We don't water down the gospel. We do not rely on our cleverness or our strategizing to manage them.

Paul says the cross abolishes our foolishness. And yet, foolishly, we often see ourselves as somehow innocent, in the right, unlike others. In doing so, don't we risk emptying the cross of its power—its power for us? People convinced of their own innocence cannot be reconciled. This is what Trocmé learned while preaching to both the French and the Germans. Only the repentant can be reconciled. Only the repentant can partake of the power of forgiveness and new life through Christ's cross.

So how do we participate in the ministry of Christ so that the cross is not emptied of its power? I think we do what Christ does through its power: we love across the differences in the places God sends his church. We love among and across the difference, not negating differences or reducing them to a power struggle. We love across them and in them, even if we do so poorly, imperfectly. We suffer them; we bear their burden; we give thanks for them. This is the power of the cross. For the cross of Jesus Christ is the shape of divine loving, embracing, suffering, and—most of all—redeeming and transforming creaturely difference. There is no other.

Isn't this what Christ himself did? And, now that he is ascended, what he continues to do? He loves across the largest difference of all, the largest division of all, the largest power struggle of all in order to reach God's own creation, with all its creaturely distinctions—broken, disobedient, rebellious, lost. God who creates us, loves and longs for us, looks at his creation and doesn't see it as we do, as this group and that, as friend and foe, as liberal and conservative. God looks on all of us with our many divisions and only sees his children, whoever we are, lost, far away from him and each other. So he sent us Jesus to give his life for all of us, to bring us all home, back to him, to make us one. He calls us all his sisters and brothers. We know this, don't we? We wouldn't be here if this single love, which has loved us across the chasm between ourselves and God, hadn't claimed us.

And so God sends his church to all nations, to live and witness in such a way that the cross is not emptied of its power. And lives are changed. Because of this we come to Wycliffe. Here, hopefully, our eyes will be trained to see the world and ourselves through the single light of the cross. And our hearts and lives will continue to take on the concrete shape of God's own embrace and suffering of our differences. It is an audacious thing we do, isn't it? I hope we do so with seriousness and humility. And with hope and joy. For in God's foolish wisdom God sends people—you, me, and all the other folks who cause this world terrible problems—as his witnesses. In his foolish wisdom, God sends people like us to the ends of the earth, people who find it so hard to love those who are different. And yet God sends us to do just this. Doesn't he have a better plan? This *is* his plan. And so in God's foolish wisdom, he sends his church to all nations—near and far, to friend and stranger—to live and witness and love, in such a way that the cross of Jesus Christ is not emptied of its power. Imagine.

Amen.

Third Sermon Example: Psalm 24; Isaiah 25:6–9; John 11:32–44; Revelation 21:1–6a

A word about context and form: I preached this in the local congregation I serve. It is culturally diverse and in a neighborhood of multiple immigrant groups, many of whom are new to Toronto. The church has strong ties in the community. I try to adopt a tone that is somewhat colloquial as a way to invite inquiry without, I hope, detracting from the power and inspiration of the text. I quickly move into the Gospel narrative and stick with it through the sermon. The form of the sermon is shaped by the narrative. It is an inductive sermon, though I step out of this form at times, especially toward the end. The noninductive sections serve to interpret points I gleaned inductively. In my retelling of the Gospel text, I use questions to keep my congregation moving with me.

Question 1: What Do I See? The Preacher as Witness

▶ **Main action:** Attentively read the appointed Scriptures.

The appointed Gospel (John 11:32–44) is part of the larger story of Lazarus. The Gospel has a complex movement. On one hand, it is a linear narrative, but it refers to events that have already taken place in the story of the illness and death of Lazarus and the ministry of Jesus, such as the healing of the blind man (v. 37) and an earlier conversation with Martha about seeing God's glory (v. 40). Jesus thanks the Father for having heard him in the past (vv. 41–42).

Jesus speaks to four different people or groups: Martha (vv. 39–40), his Father in heaven (vv. 41–42), Lazarus (v. 43), and "them"—the sisters and the crowd (v. 44). Lazarus never speaks, here or in the mention of him in chapter 12.

Lazarus is called out of the tomb—a place where he has been cut off from others—and into the middle of the crowd, which includes Jesus, family, friends, and skeptics. He sees Jesus face-to-face with these others around, and all of them, including the skeptics, witness his return to life. Jesus doesn't unbind Lazarus's burial clothes. He asks others to do it. All of this is independent of Lazarus's wishes, as far as we know. Lazarus never speaks and did not request to be raised (nor did the dry bones of Israel). Jesus connects this with his glory (*kabod*, *doxa*). My eye catches the focus on glory in the larger gospel story of Lazarus and Psalm 24.

The image of the raised Lazarus standing in front of Jesus leads me to Job's declaration of the promise, "I know that my Redeemer lives, and that at the last day . . . in my flesh I shall see God" (Job 19:25–26).

I follow Jesus's prayer of thanks to his Father for having heard him and his declaration that he says this for the sake of the crowd (John 11:41–42) to other places where Jesus prays to his Father or one of them speaks for the sake of the crowds or disciples (see Matt. 3:17; 11:25–26; 14:23; 17:5; Mark 1:11, 35; Luke 6:12; 22:32; John 12:27–28; 17:1–26; Heb. 5:7; 2 Pet. 1:17).

The promise to Martha that she would see God's glory (11:40) and the reference to it in 11:4 leads me back to the appointed psalm, where Jesus is described as the King of glory (24:7–10). It also leads me to the declaration that Moses cannot see God's glory and live (Exod. 33:20) and to the beginning of John's Gospel, which declares, "We have seen his glory, the glory as of a father's only son" (1:14). It also leads, of course, to the description of Christ's death as glorification in the rest of John's Gospel.

The tomb, the stone, and the burial strips of cloth lead me to Jesus's tomb, death, and resurrection. There is a striking difference regarding movement. In the appointed Gospel, the central actions happen at Jesus's command: "Take away the stone"; "come out"; "unbind him, and let him go." These same actions take place at Jesus's resurrection, but we do not see them occur or overhear the command or action that makes them occur. No one witnesses these actions, only their aftermath. In the raising of Lazarus and the dry bones, there are witnesses.

Question 2: Whom Do I See? The Preacher as Witness to Christ

▶ **Main action:** Describe the identity of Jesus Christ revealed in the text.

In this passage, Jesus does many things. He responds publicly to the death of a loved one and declares that it is for the sake of the crowd. He commands both the living and the dead: take away the stone; come out; unbind him. He speaks to his Father. He thanks him for always hearing. He promises Martha that she will see his glory if she believes. He speaks to his Father so the crowds will believe that the Father has sent him. He raises Lazarus from the dead.

Jesus is the one who raises the dead, whether or not they ask for it. He is the one who creates witnesses to his power to do so. He is the one who tells us, the church, that unbinding burial clothes is our vocation. Jesus is the Son of the God of Israel, sent to respond to our deaths through his own death and resurrection, which is God's glory, so we may see Christ face-to-face and witness to it during our lives and after our resurrections. In short, Jesus is the resurrected one for us.

Question 3: What Is Christ's Word to Me? The Preacher as Confessor

▶ **Main action:** Hear God's address to you and receive God's mercy and judgment.

I hear Jesus telling me that others are there to help me unbind the clothes of my old self. I hear him telling me that is what he does—commands others to unbind the clothes that hold me to the old life he has replaced with his resurrected life. Somehow this is connected to his glory. He asks me, "Why do you not turn to the ones I send you?" He tells me that I turn away from him and his new life when I keep trying to change my own burial clothes. That is not what he or Lazarus did. In this I hear his offer of mercy, which I find difficult to receive. Do I hear his judgment in my rejection of his mercy? I also hear him telling me that I am a witness to resurrection—his own and others' through his. I can't avoid this fact.

Question 4: What Is Christ's Word to Us? The Preacher as Theologian

▶ **Main action:** Hear God's address to the church and one's own congregation in its particular context.

I heard Jesus tell us this: "I have given all of you what I gave Lazarus—new life through my Word. It is only through my Word, only through my glory, my death and resurrection for you and all creation. There is no life rising from the dead apart from me. Because you all are bound to me in this life, you are bound to each other as well. This is my glory. The new life I give you is not just for yourselves, as Lazarus's was not just for him. It is so you can witness to who I am. That is why I command you to unbind the burial clothes of each other and to allow others to do so for you."

Question 5: What Is Christ's Word about Us? The Preacher as Theologian of a Broken Body

▶ **Main action:** Describe the identity of the church and the disciple given in Christ's word and address to us.

We are witnesses to what Jesus does, which is to raise the dead to new life. We are recipients of this new life, through our baptisms into his death and resurrection and through our faith in him. We are the ones he commands to unbind the burial clothes of others, as we let others unbind ours. In doing so, we are the ones who show the world, through these actions, what it is like to live the new life given in him. We are the ones he calls to make this visible—among friends, family, fellow believers, and skeptics. People see his glory when you make it visible.

Question 6: What Does It Look Like? The Preacher as Witness to Christ in a Disobedient World

▶ **Main action:** Facilitate recognition of how the identity of Christ is inhabited in a broken and disobedient world.

During the week I was reminded of a story. A group of church members had known each other for many years in the community, in the church, and in a Bible study they attended together. They differed politically, theologically, and economically. They had in common their stubbornness, which added to the friction. One member was an elderly retired nurse, the other a set of doctors, still practicing. Over the years the elderly woman, who lived alone, became more frail and unable to care for herself and her many animals. We had a relationship with her daughter, who lived in another city. Toward the end of her life and the several hospitalizations that were part of it, the city removed her many cats, but she still had an old, ugly dog, which she could not care for properly. At her deathbed, the other parishioners in the Bible study, who had been at odds with her all these years, offered to take her dog as their own when she died.

I need to remove my emotional attachment to these parishioners to determine whether to use this story. The point is not my affection but the function of the story. The core of the story is the willingness of the parishioners to adopt the old dog of this dying woman who annoyed them. That this story happens at the time of her death and extends beyond her death is important to me because it points to a bond in Christ that extends beyond death. I know there are many dog lovers in the congregation, so I will avoid describing it as ugly (though it was). They would probably stop listening at that point.

The parishioners who adopted this dog recognized that in Christ they had a connection to this woman, which bound them to her despite their mutual dislike. They knew that Jesus had given eternal life to both them and this woman. They had a bond with her beyond death. They were able to see Jesus as the giver of bonds despite our disobedience (here, their inability to get along with her) and despite death. They chose to bind themselves to her, in response to who they were together in Christ, by adopting her dog.

This dog was really old, ugly, and pitiful, but these parishioners were wild about him, sweet and tender with him, and provided the care he needed after being neglected. When I saw this love, I recognized something of God's glory in the dog. I saw Jesus, whose love creates beauty in what is old, broken, and discarded.

In this small story we see that through this woman's death, the clothes of the couple's hardened hearts were unbound in the adoption of the woman's dog. As Christians, we are people who stay bound to others, despite difficulty, in Jesus's bond to us. The story tells us that we are Christ's followers despite our failures. It shows that the church's vocation in all times and ages is to continually listen to Christ's call to unbind the burial clothes that hold us, the church, and this world to our old lives.

I think I will use the story for the sermon (once I get permission), but carefully. It would be easy to sentimentalize it and thus the gospel. It is a small story, and I need to keep it small and prevent it from displacing the gospel story. I will make sure I return to the Gospel text after I tell it. From the Gospel story and this story, I have reflected on both God's glory and Christ's command to unbind the burial clothes, two rich images around which I could structure a sermon. Because both are rich, I don't think it is effective to focus on both in one sermon. I think I will go with glory and use the sermon story to point to what God's glory looks like—caring for an old dog!

Sermon on John 11:38–44

Lazarus is dead. His sisters are weeping. Friends and neighbors have come to their house with their casseroles and cakes. Every group of people has customs surrounding death. At the very least, these rituals of food and phone calls, texts and stopping by, keep us busy. They give us something to do when the bottom falls out of our lives.

That's what's going on after the death of Lazarus. The house is full, neighbors coming and going. John writes that in the middle of this, Mary quickly gets up and leaves her house. The crowd thinks she's going to Lazarus's tomb to weep over her dead brother, and they follow. But Mary surprises them. Instead, she goes out to meet Jesus, whose arrival has been delayed. "If you had been here, my brother would not have died," she says to him (John 11:32). She's crying, her neighbors and friends are crying, and so is Jesus. They all go together to see his tomb: Mary, Jesus, the crowd from her house, folks they pick up along the way, small children from the village. It's a mixed group gathered around Lazarus's tomb. John describes it for us. Some are moved by Jesus. "See how he loved him," they say (v. 36). Some are, at best, skeptical. "Could not he who opened the eyes of the blind man have kept this man from dying?" (v. 37). Some probably have never heard of Jesus. It's a mixed crowd, like any family or town. Like any funeral crowd.

Lazarus's tomb is a cave with a stone laid in front of it. It's a lot like the one that will shortly be Jesus's own. By this time, Martha, Lazarus's other sister, has joined the growing and weeping crowd at the tomb. "Take away the stone," Jesus says to Martha. "It's been four days, Jesus," Martha says. "It will smell terrible" (11:39). In response to her protest, Jesus says something that seems out of place in this story of grief and loss, neighbors, stench and tears. He says, "Did I not tell you that if you believed, you would see the glory of God?" (v. 40). If you believed, you would see the glory of God.

Here? In a tomb with a four-day-old corpse, Jesus tells us we are going to see God's glory? It's not surprising, is it, that John tells us that some members of the crowd were skeptical. So here's my question for us. Help me answer it. Where in this story do we see God's glory? We talk about God's glory all the time in church. *The whole earth is full of his glory*, we sing. Our psalm today names Jesus as the King of glory. Glory is something we can see or at least apprehend. It is the reality of God, of who God is for the world, made visible. His powerful love brings into existence what is not, brings new life out of our broken lives and world, and brings about his purposes for creation. His glory is this life-giving love made visible. So, back to my question: Where in this story do we see this—God's glory? And here's a second question that is important to ask for those of us who try to respond to God's love as we go about our days: What are we supposed to do with what we see?

Back to the story. After telling Martha that if she believes she will see God's glory, Jesus prays to his Father. It's an odd prayer, don't you think? Because Jesus doesn't pray for dead Lazarus. He doesn't pray for his heart-broken sisters. He doesn't even pray for himself. Instead he prays on behalf of the folks who seem the least in need of prayer: the crowd—the whole motley group—who have left their casseroles and cakes in Mary's house and followed her and Jesus to Lazarus's tomb. Listen to what Jesus prays: "Father, I knew that you always hear me, but I have said this *for the sake of the crowd* standing here, so that they may believe that you sent me" (11:42).

He prays for them and then responds to the situation that has brought them to this tomb: Lazarus's death. You know what Jesus does. With a loud voice he cries, "Lazarus, come out!" (11:43). What happens? The stone has been rolled away, and in response to Jesus's voice, Lazarus, who had died, comes out. He is in his burial clothes, which are strips of cloth bound around his hands, face, and feet. Then Jesus does this: With Lazarus standing in front of him, bound in his burial clothes, Jesus turns to the crowd. He turns to the gathered crowd of family, believers, skeptics, and everyone else—that is, those on whose behalf he has just prayed. He turns to *them* and says, "Unbind him, and let him go" (v. 44).

There is something odd about Jesus calling to Lazarus in a loud voice, isn't there? "Lazarus, come out!" Can dead men hear? Could Lazarus hear Jesus's voice any more than the dry bones of Israel could hear Ezekiel preaching to them? Is this where we see God's glory? Yes, certainly. God's Word creates life out of nothing, just as God spoke into the formless void and brought about the heavens and earth out of nothing. Here that same Word made flesh speaks into the tomb of the dead Lazarus. Out of nothing, out of death itself, God brings life. Isn't this who Jesus is—the resurrected one for all of us? How could this be anything other than God's glory seen in Jesus?

Now, there is more to the story, another detail so obvious that we move right past it. When Lazarus comes out from the tomb, where does he stand? Where does he stand? Luke tells us. He *stands* before the one who has called to him, Jesus. He *stands* before the one to whom the Father always listens. He *stands, given new life,* before the one the Father sent. But this is not all, is it? He stands before the crowd, which has followed Mary from her house to the tomb. The crowd, which includes family, onlookers, believers, skeptics, the neighborhood kids, and everyone in between. The crowd Jesus has just prayed for and has instructed to unbind Lazarus—Lazarus stands before them as well. Lazarus stands in front of everyone gathered around his tomb who has seen the glory of God.

So can you see what's going on? The new life Jesus gives Lazarus is not just for him, grateful as he might be. Or for his sisters. Or even for those who believe in Jesus. It is for everyone there. Sisters, skeptics, neighbors, and kids see in Lazarus the promise Jesus makes to us. The promise is this: after our deaths, we will stand, like Lazarus, before the one the Father has sent, Jesus Christ. Because through his own death, Jesus has made death a servant of life.

This promise is our hope. It is the hope of God's people across time, made first to Israel, and from Israel to the church, and from the church to all nations. It is the hope that carries us through the burial of our dead. We proclaim this as we bury them: "I know that my Redeemer liveth and that he shall stand at the latter day upon the earth; and though this body be destroyed, yet I shall see God, whom I shall see for myself and mine eyes shall behold, who is a friend and not a stranger."[15]

So is this it as well? God's glory? How could it not be? Seeing God face-to-face and realizing he is a friend and no stranger. Yes, our recognition of Christ as friend will certainly be glorious. Ah, but the story of Lazarus gives us an even fuller picture of what God's glory will look like. And it helps us answer the second question I asked: When we see God's glory—now—what are we supposed to do with it? How do we respond?

How many of us have asked the following question to someone who (we hope) can give us an answer? When we die, will we see our loved ones? Will I see my wife? My brother who died as a child? Will I get to see my best friend? Today, here, Jesus answers that question. Lazarus stands before Jesus, who is his friend and not a stranger (Job 19:27). But he stands there *also* with the crowd that brought cakes and casseroles to Mary's house and then followed her to his tomb. With the ones who witnessed the whole thing. With the ones Jesus tells to unbind Lazarus from his burial clothes. With the ones Jesus prays for. At the resurrection of the dead, will we see our loved ones? Jesus's answer: Yes, yes indeed—and not only your loved ones but your loved ones and those not so easy to love.

Here is the fullness of God's glory for us to apprehend. When we stand before God after our deaths, we will not stand alone. We will stand with the risen and ascended Christ. We will stand with our loved ones. And not only with our loved ones. Isn't this, as Paul says in Ephesians 2, what Jesus came, lived, died, and rose for? To draw all people to himself? Isn't this why, through his death, he broke down the dividing walls of hostility between peoples, made friends of strangers, neighbors of those who had been far off? Isn't this what the Father sent him for, so that all things—all things in heaven and earth—may be made one in him? So it's not surprising that when Lazarus stands before the one who has given him new life, a crowd gathers around him. Those he loves are there, to be sure; but as we heard, not only them. You see, right here—as Lazarus stands in front of Jesus, surrounded by the others—God points us to the place we are to

15. *Book of Common Prayer*, Burial of the Dead: Rite II (Toronto: Anglican Book Centre, 1962), 491; cf. Job 19:25–26.

look to see God's glory. That place includes where we stand *now* and not only with our loved ones. Where we stand with neighbors, skeptics, kids, with those who share our faith, with those who scoff at it, and with those who have never heard of Jesus.

I realize now that I once saw God's glory in the strangest place: in an old, half-blind dog. I had parishioners in a long-standing Bible study who found it almost impossible to love each other. They'd known each other for years. One was a cranky, opinionated elderly woman who had been a nurse, and the others were an equally opinionated, somewhat inflexible couple, both doctors. They were at odds on everything: politics, the church, health care—all of which came out in the Bible study. Toward the end of her life, the elderly woman grew too weak to care for her dog. Her daughter couldn't take him. She was distraught. This couple, who had sparred with her for so long, took her dog. They cared for it for the rest of its life. Each time I saw that dog, now well-fed and groomed—each time I saw how happy that dog made them—I think I saw God's glory. Why? Remember the promise Jesus makes to Martha when she tells him her brother is dead? "Did I not tell you that if you believed, you would see the glory of God?" This couple knew they were bound to this difficult woman in Christ. They knew that death didn't get them off the hook. We didn't do so well with getting along, they told me. But here they were, still bound to this difficult woman through her old, half-blind dog. And loving him. That is what glory looks like, I think.

Now, if I can see God's glory in such a small act, imagine what is possible. Right here. As we stand now—not after our deaths—as we stand now with those we will stand with eternally. With those we find difficult to love. With those the world finds expendable. We don't stand with them because it's the right thing to do—that won't get us very far. We stand with them because, with Mary and Martha, we believe Jesus is the resurrected one and he has bound us together, which means we are stuck with each other, now and after our deaths. Isn't this why Christ has given us his life, so we have the strength and grace to stand with others, instead of ignoring them or running away? We stand and, joined to Christ, are not pushed over or knocked aside.

What about those who live around our church, on this corner? Do they see God's glory through us? What about our kids? They're always watching. And our colleagues and friends? God's glory? None of them will use that term. But we know what it is and where to look to see it. So if God gives us the eyes to recognize who will be standing with us when we see Jesus face-to-face—and there is going to be a crowd—don't you think God wants us to begin to get to know them now? And love them now? In Christ we are already bound to them eternally. Believe it, he says to us, as he said to Martha. Believe it and begin to get to know them now. Stand with them now and you will be witnesses to my glory.

Amen.

Conclusion

Love as the Hermeneutical Criterion

I recently spent time with the three-year-old son of my niece. Like many young children, he loves trucks. Or any vehicle found in the public works division of a major city. His love is evidenced in two ways. First, he spends a lot of time playing with them, moving them around and making all their attendant sounds. Second, he knows the names of all of them and their various parts. Backhoe, cement mixer with drum, bulldozer with or without ripper, and so on. I have wanted to learn the names of all the trees in the park across the street from my college. I haven't done it yet. I have not spent the time, nor quite frankly desired it deeply enough, to give it the attention needed.

We cannot love what we do not know. As preachers, we have bound ourselves to God's Word and God's people for the sake of God and the world God so loves. The form of this binding is a single, attentive gaze: the practice of looking again rather than looking away. In this life, God's truth and transforming power are held *only* in transient wrappers: the difficult words of Scripture, our feeble sermons, our broken people, our flawed church, this violent world. But we are mistaken if we forget just what these commonplace vessels hold: the power of God, through the death and resurrection of Jesus Christ, to set the world aright. Paul reminds us, "But we have this treasure in clay jars, so that it may be made clear that this extraordinary power belongs to God and does not come from us" (2 Cor. 4:7).

165

In Christ's embrace of creaturely limitations, God has made these broken vessels both the road and the end to which they lead, Jesus Christ, the power and wisdom of God (1 Cor. 1:24). Here we find our vocation as preachers: to live within the fleshly constraints of the human condition with hope. The promise is that over time the eyes of our hearts will be enlightened so we may see the riches of God's promises for this broken world (Eph. 1:18).

I know of no other hope for the world than Jesus Christ. The 2016 US presidential election revealed a country that has lost the ability to listen across divides. This is not limited to the United States. Far more troubling is the loss of an urgent sense of the need for doing so. In a complicated, global, and violent world, we have retreated into echo chambers of our own small, constructed realities. But in his incarnation, Christ has become our neighbor. God moved into a place he does not belong and made it his own. Christ's descent into a place he did not belong moves us to direct our gaze toward others, toward our neighbor, in love. In a world of increasingly contested realities, we refuse to use others as either instruments or obstacles. We are called to know them so we may love them, to bear the burden of their freedom as Christ bears ours in love. We do not flee from the world of our neighbors, the temporal, and the contingent. We do not need to. Christ gives us the skills needed to stick with both the textually mediated world of Scripture and the fleshly limitations of the human condition—and an ability to see the redemption of both in his incarnation. Love is the hermeneutical criterion in both overlapping spheres.[1]

God has made it so. God's plan for the fullness of time binds us to one another. He has called his church to preach. God has entrusted the salvation of the world to the foolishness of our preaching (1 Cor. 1:21). As Augustine has written, God has "sanctioned the homage of the human voice" to speak of him who is unspeakable.[2] He continues, "The human condition would be wretched indeed if God appeared unwilling to minister his word to human beings through human agency. . . . Moreover, there would be no way for love, which ties people together in the bonds of unity, to make souls overflow and as it were intermingle with each other, if human beings learned nothing from

---

1. I am grateful to Paul Kolbet for this phrase from *Augustine and the Cure of Souls*, 150.
2. Augustine, *On Christian Teaching* 1.14.

other humans."[3] Firsthand experience, as Charles Williams writes, is entrusted to second-rate preaching.[4] This is the way of love.

I have argued that a quick exit from Scripture's room is unnecessary. To remain within it, with a compass for its navigation, is far less of a burden on the preacher than erecting one unsteady bridge of meaning after another. This practice invites preachers to listen to the textually fixed discourse of Scripture as God's personal and corporate address to the church across time, heard and interpreted in one's own context. Rather than a retreat into a kind of historical universalism, this approach offers a renewed description of the correlation of scriptural texts and the current world of its hearers. It is located in God's continuous purposes for creation, as rendered in the Spirit's use of Scripture in the church. This practice returns Scripture to its natural habitat, the church, in which both the text and listeners are rooted and where the Word is textually and contextually mediated, echoed, and embodied in the church's practices. Reading Scripture intratextually, paying attention to its ascriptive logic, and employing a communal hermeneutic, along with one's own exegetical work—each offers a way to linger in Scripture's room, to listen with and on behalf of one's people, and to preach. My hope is that the Holy Spirit uses the weekly task of sermon preparation for God's ongoing formation of his tired preachers, and through them the people with whom they live.

There is a need for theologians and biblical scholars to join homileticians in sustained reflection on the church's preaching. Asking questions about what various approaches to preaching express relative to Christology, ecclesiology, anthropology, discipleship, and Scripture's inspiration is central to the vocation of the theologian to serve the church. The development of guidelines for preaching, however, continues to be the task of homileticians. We need coherent, accessible guidelines that will help preachers know how to listen to Scripture with their congregations, how to interpret it theologically, and how to move from interpretation to proclamation. How do we help preachers proclaim the good news of Jesus Christ to divided churches and communities? My hope is that these

---

3. Augustine, preface to *On Christian Teaching* 1.13–14, pp. 5–6.

4. Charles Williams, *Descent of the Dove: A Short History of the Holy Spirit in the Church* (Eugene, OR: Wipf and Stock, 2016), 170.

guidelines are both theologically sound and simple enough to be used toward that end.

The goal of holding theology and practice together is characteristically Anglican. An Anglican focus on external forms is based on the conviction of Christ's transforming presence in them, when those forms—worship, prayer, the practices of the church—are Scripture's own. By asking a series of specific questions of Scripture, the Six Questions of the Sermon invite the preacher to read it with her congregation through a particular hermeneutical lens. This is no accident. If how we pray shapes how we believe, then, at the least, how we read Scripture shapes how we preach.

The shape of our sermons is Jesus Christ. He is the foolishness of our preaching, the Word made flesh, which is the salvation of the world (1 Cor. 1:21). In Christ's humanity God adapted his Word to our specific context, to our dull ears and weak perceptive powers. In Christ's humanity God's Word speaks to us in humble eloquence, and through this same Word the Spirit gives us the ears to listen and eyes to recognize what sin has made us unable to see or hear on our own. Our response is a life shaped by Christ's own. An identity we receive rather than construct. An identity and vocation found *within* Christ's embrace.

Further Reading

Sermon Collections and Essays

Boersma, Hans. *Sacramental Preaching: Sermons on the Hidden Presence of Christ.* Grand Rapids: Baker Academic, 2016.

Davis, Ellen F., and Austin McIver Dennis, foreword by Stanley Hauerwas. *Preaching the Luminous Word: Biblical Sermons and Homiletical Essays.* Grand Rapids: Eerdmans, 2016.

Dean, Robert J., foreword by Fleming Rutledge. *Leaps of Faith: Sermons from the Edge.* Eugene, OR: Resource Publications, 2017.

Rutledge, Fleming. *And God Spoke to Abraham: Preaching from the Old Testament.* Grand Rapids: Eerdmans, 2011.

Simmons, Martha, and Frank A. Thomas, eds., foreword by Gardner C. Taylor. *Preaching with Sacred Fire: An Anthology of African American Sermons, 1750 to the Present.* New York: W. W. Norton, 2010.

Theological Interpretation of Scripture

Bartholomew, Craig G., and David J. H. Beldman, eds. *Hearing the Old Testament: Listening for God's Address.* Grand Rapids: Eerdmans, 2012.

Billings, J. Todd. *The Word of God for the People of God: An Entryway to the Theological Interpretation of Scripture*. Grand Rapids: Eerdmans, 2010.

Boersma, Hans. *Scripture as Real Presence: Sacramental Exegesis in the Early Church*. Grand Rapids: Baker Academic, 2017.

Davis, Ellen F., and Richard B. Hays, eds. *The Art of Reading Scripture*. Grand Rapids: Eerdmans, 2003.

Reno, R. R. *Brazos Theological Commentary on the Bible*. 20 vols. Grand Rapids: Brazos, 2005–.

Seitz, Christopher R. *Word Without End: The Old Testament as Abiding Theological Witness*. Old Testament Studies. Grand Rapids: Eerdmans, 2002.

Treier, Daniel J. *Introducing Theological Interpretation of Scripture: Recovering a Christian Practice*. Grand Rapids: Baker Academic, 2008.

Preaching and the Role of the Preacher

Campbell, Charles L. *The Word before the Powers: An Ethic of Preaching*. Louisville, KY: Westminster John Knox, 2002.

Vanhoozer, Kevin J., and Owen Strachan. *The Pastor as Public Theologian: Reclaiming a Lost Vision*. Grand Rapids: Baker Academic, 2015.

Bibliography

Abraham, William. "On Making Disciples of the Lord Jesus Christ." In *Marks of the Body of Christ*, edited by Carl E. Braaten and Robert W. Jenson, 150–66. Grand Rapids: Eerdmans, 1999.

Achtemeier, Elizabeth. *Creative Preaching: Finding the Words*. Nashville: Abingdon, 1980.

Allen, O. Wesley. *Determining the Form: Structures for Preaching*. Elements of Preaching. Minneapolis: Fortress, 2008.

———, ed. *The Renewed Homiletic*. Minneapolis: Fortress, 2010.

Allen, Ronald J. *Preaching and the Other: Studies of Postmodern Insights*. St. Louis: Chalice, 2009.

Auden, W. H. *Collected Poems*. Edited by Edward Mendelson. New York: Random House, 2007.

Auerbach, Erich. *Mimesis: The Representation of Reality in Western Literature*. Translated by Willard R. Trask. Princeton: Princeton University Press, 1968.

Augustine. *Confessions*. New York: Penguin, 1961.

———. *Essential Sermons*. Edited by Daniel E. Doyle. Hyde Park, NY: New City, 2007.

———. *On Christian Teaching (On Christian Doctrine)*. Translated by R. P. H. Green. Oxford: Oxford University Press, 1999.

———. *Sermons (1–19) on the Old Testament*. Part 3, vol. 8 of *The Works of St. Augustine: A Translation for the Twenty-First Century*. Translated by Edmund Hill. Edited by John E. Rotelle. Hyde Park, NY: New City, 1990.

———. *Sermons to the People: Advent, Christmas, New Year's, Epiphany*. Edited and translated by William Griffin. New York: Image/Doubleday, 2002.

Balthasar, Hans Urs von. *Truth Is Symphonic: Aspects of Christian Pluralism*. Translated by Graham Harrison. San Francisco: Ignatius, 1987.

Barter Moulaison, Jane. *Lord, Giver of Life: Toward a Pneumatological Complement to George Lindbeck's Theory of Doctrine*. Waterloo, ON:

Wilfrid Laurier University Press, 2007.

Barth, Karl. *Church Dogmatics*, 4 vols. Edited by G. W. Bromiley and T. F. Torrance. New York: T&T Clark, 2009.

———. *Homiletics* Translated by Geoffrey W. Bromiley and Donald E. Daniels. Louisville: Westminster John Knox, 1991.

Bartholomew, Craig G., and David J. H. Beldman. *Hearing the Old Testament: Listening for God's Address.* Grand Rapids: Eerdmans, 2012.

Bass, Dorothy C. *Practicing Our Faith: A Way of Life for a Searching People.* San Francisco: Jossey-Bass, 1997.

Bass, George. "The Evolution of the Story Sermon." *Word & World* 2, no. 2 (1982): 183–89, https://wordandworld.luthersem.edu/content/pdfs/2-2_Kingdom/2-2_Bass.pdf.

Bauckham, Richard. *Jesus and the Eyewitnesses: The Gospels as Eyewitness Testimony.* Grand Rapids: Eerdmans, 2008.

Billings, J. Todd. *The Word of God for the People of God: An Entryway to the Theological Interpretation of Scripture.* Grand Rapids: Eerdmans, 2010.

Blount, Brian, and Lenora Tubbs Tisdale, eds. *Making Room at the Table: An Invitation to Multicultural Worship.* Louisville: Westminster John Knox, 2001.

Boismorand, Pierre, ed. *Magda and André Trocmé: Resistance Figures.* Translated by Jo-Anne Elder. Montreal: McGill-Queen's University Press, 2014.

Bonhoeffer, Dietrich. *Life Together: The Classic Exploration of Christian Community.* Translated by John W. Doberstein. New York: Harper & Row, 1954.

Book of Common Prayer. Toronto: Anglican Book Centre, 1962.

Booty, John. *Reflections on the Theology of Richard Hooker: An Elizabethan Addresses Modern Anglicanism.* Sewanee, TN: University of the South Press, 1998.

———. "Richard Hooker and the Holy Scriptures." *SEAD* Occasional Paper 3 (May 1995): 1–13.

Braaten, Carl, and Robert W. Jenson, eds. *Marks of the Body of Christ.* Grand Rapids: Eerdmans, 1999.

———. *Principles of Lutheran Theology.* 2nd ed. Minneapolis: Fortress, 2007.

Breidenthal, Thomas. "Sharper Than a Two-Edged Sword: Following the Logic of the Text in Preaching." In *Sharper Than a Two-Edged Sword: Preaching, Teaching and Living the Bible*, edited by Michael Root and James J. Buckley, 32–43. Grand Rapids: Eerdmans, 2008.

Brooks, Phillips. *Eight Lectures on Preaching.* London: SPCK, 1959.

Brown, Peter. *Augustine of Hippo: A Biography.* Rev. ed. Berkeley: University of California Press, 2000.

Brueggemann, Walter. *The Word That Redescribes the World: The Bible and Discipleship.* Minneapolis: Fortress, 2006.

Buckley, James J., and David S. Yeago, eds. *Knowing the Triune God: The Work of the Spirit in the Practices of the Church.* Grand Rapids: Eerdmans, 2001.

Burghardt, Walter J. *Hear the Just Word and Live It.* New York: Paulist Press, 2000.

Buschart, W. David, and Ken D. Eilers. *Theology as Retrieval: Receiving the Past, Renewing the Church.*

Downers Grove, IL: IVP Academic, 2015.

Buttrick, David. *Homiletic: Moves and Structures*. Philadelphia: Fortress, 1988.

———. "Interpretation and Preaching." *Interpretation* 35, no. 1 (January 1981): 46–58.

Campbell, Charles L. "Performing the Scriptures: Preaching and Jesus' 'Third Way.'" *Journal for Preachers* 17, no. 2 (Lent 1994): 18–24.

———. *Preaching Jesus: New Directions for Homiletics in Hans Frei's Postliberal Theology*. Grand Rapids: Eerdmans, 1997.

———. *The Word before the Powers: An Ethic of Preaching*. Louisville: Westminster John Knox, 2002.

Chapell, Bryan. "When Narrative Is Not Enough." *Presbyterian* 22, no. 1 (1996): 3–16.

Chapman, Raymond, ed. *Law and Revelation: Richard Hooker and His Writings*. Canterbury Studies in Spiritual Theology. Norwich: Canterbury Press, 2009.

Clapp, Rodney. *A Peculiar People: The Church as Culture in a Post-Christian Society*. Downers Grove, IL: InterVarsity, 1996.

Colish, Marcia. *The Mirror of Language: A Study in the Medieval Theory of Knowledge*. Rev. ed. Lincoln: University of Nebraska Press, 1983.

Cooper, Burton. *Claiming Theology in the Pulpit*. Louisville: Westminster John Knox, 2003.

Daniel, Lillian. *Tell It Like It Is: Reclaiming the Practice of Testimony*. Lanham, MD: Rowman & Littlefield, 2006.

Davis, Ellen F. *Imagination Shaped: Old Testament Preaching and the Anglican Tradition*. Valley Forge, PA: Trinity Press International, 1995.

———. "Teaching the Bible Confessionally in the Church." In *The Art of Reading Scripture*, edited by Ellen F. Davis and Richard B. Hays, 9–26. Grand Rapids: Eerdmans, 2003.

———. *Wondrous Depth: Preaching the Old Testament*. Louisville: Westminster John Knox, 2005.

Davis, Ellen F., and Richard B. Hays, eds. *The Art of Reading Scripture*. Grand Rapids: Eerdmans, 2003.

———. "Learning to Read the Bible Again." *Christian Century*, April 20, 2004, 23–24.

Demson, David. *Hans Frei and Karl Barth: Different Ways of Reading Scripture*. Grand Rapids: Eerdmans, 1997.

Dunn-Wilson, David. *A Mirror for the Church: Preaching in the First Five Centuries*. Grand Rapids: Eerdmans, 2005.

Edwards, O. C. *A History of Preaching*. Nashville: Abingdon, 2004.

Ellingsen, Mark. *The Integrity of Biblical Narrative*. Minneapolis: Fortress, 1990.

Eslinger, Richard. *Intersections: Post-Critical Studies in Preaching*. Grand Rapids: Eerdmans, 1994.

———. *Narrative and Imagination: Preaching the Worlds That Shape Us*. Minneapolis: Fortress, 1995.

———. *A New Hearing: Living Options in Homiletic Method*. Nashville: Abingdon, 1987.

———. *The Web of Preaching: New Options in Homiletical Method*. Nashville: Abingdon, 2002.

Farley, Edward. "Preaching the Bible and Preaching the Gospel."

Theology Today 51, no. 1 (April 1994): 90–103.

Farris, Stephen. "Limping Away with a Blessing: Biblical Studies and Preaching at the End of the Second Millennium." *Interpretation* 51, no. 4 (1997): 358–70.

Fish, Stanley. *How to Write a Sentence: And How to Read One.* New York: HarperCollins, 2011.

———. *Is There a Text in This Class? The Authority of Interpretive Communities.* Cambridge, MA: Harvard University Press, 1980.

Fitzgerald, Allan D. *Augustine through the Ages: An Encyclopedia.* Grand Rapids: Eerdmans, 1999.

Florence, Anna Carter. *Preaching as Testimony.* Louisville: Westminster John Knox, 2007.

Forde, Gerhard O. *Theology Is for Proclamation.* Minneapolis: Augsburg Fortress, 1990.

———. "The Word That Kills and Makes Alive." In *Marks of the Body of Christ,* edited by Carl E. Braaten and Robert W. Jenson, 1–12. Grand Rapids: Eerdmans, 1999.

Fowl, Stephen. *Engaging Scripture: A Model for Theological Interpretation.* Malden, MA: Blackwell, 1998.

Frei, Hans. *The Eclipse of Biblical Narrative: A Study in Eighteenth and Nineteenth Century Hermeneutics.* New Haven: Yale University Press, 1974.

———. *The Identity of Jesus Christ: The Hermeneutic Bases of Dogmatic Theology.* Philadelphia: Fortress, 1975.

———. "Response to 'Narrative Theology: An Evangelical Appraisal.'" *Trinity Journal* 8 (1987): 21–24.

Frye, Northrop. *The Great Code: The Bible and Literature.* Toronto: Academic Press Canada, 1982.

Fulkerson, Mary McClintock. *Changing the Subject: Women's Discourses and Feminist Theology.* Eugene, OR: Wipf and Stock, 1994.

González, Justo, and Catherine G. González. *The Liberating Pulpit.* Nashville: Abingdon, 1994.

Goppelt, Leonhard. *Typos, the Typological Interpretation of the Old Testament in the New.* Translated by Donald H. Madvig. Grand Rapids: Eerdmans, 1982.

Grady, David H. *Design for Preaching.* Philadelphia: Fortress, 1958.

Green, Joel. "The Bible, Theology and Theological Interpretation." *SBL Forum,* September 2004, https://www.sbl-site.org/publications/article.aspx?ArticleId=308.

———. *Hearing the New Testament: Strategies for Interpretation.* 2nd ed. Grand Rapids: Eerdmans, 2010.

Greene-McCreight, Kathryn. *Ad litteram: How Augustine, Calvin, and Barth Read the "Plain Sense" of Genesis 1–3.* New York: Peter Lang, 1999.

Greidanus, Sidney. *The Modern Preacher and the Ancient Text: Interpreting and Preaching Biblical Literature.* Grand Rapids: Eerdmans, 1988.

———. *Preaching Christ from Ecclesiastes: Foundations for Expository Sermons.* Grand Rapids: Eerdmans, 2010.

Gunton, Colin E. *Theology through Preaching: Sermons for Brentwood.* New York: T&T Clark, 2001.

Hatchett, Marion. *Sanctifying Life, Time and Space: An Introduction to Liturgical Study.* San Francisco: Harper & Row, 1976.

Hauerwas, Stanley. "The Church as God's New Language." In *Scriptural Authority and Narrative Interpretation*, edited by Garrett Green, 179–98. Philadelphia: Fortress, 1987.

———. *A Community of Character: Toward a Constructive Christian Social Ethic*. Notre Dame: University of Notre Dame Press, 2005.

Hauerwas, Stanley, and L. Gregory Jones, eds. *Why Narrative? Readings in Narrative Theology*. Grand Rapids: Eerdmans, 1989.

Hays, Richard B. *The Faith of Jesus Christ: The Narrative Substructure of Galatians 3:1–4:11*. Grand Rapids: Eerdmans, 2002.

Hays, Richard B., Stefan Alkier, and Leroy A. Huizenga, eds. *Reading the Bible Intertextually*. Waco: Baylor University Press, 2009.

Headley, John. *Luther's View of Church History*. New Haven: Yale University Press, 1963.

Heath, Stephen. "Intertextuality." In *A Dictionary of Cultural and Critical Theory*, edited by Michael Payne, 258–59. Oxford, UK: Blackwell, 1996.

Hill, W. Speed, and Georges Edelen, eds. *Of the Laws of Ecclesiastical Polity: Preface and Books I–IV*. Vol. 1 of *The Folger Library Edition of the Works of Richard Hooker*. Cambridge, MA: Harvard University Press, 1977.

———. *Of the Laws of Ecclesiastical Polity: Book V*. Vol. 2 of *The Folger Library Edition of the Works of Richard Hooker*. Cambridge, MA: Harvard University Press, 1977.

Hogan, Lucy Lind. "Rethinking Persuasion: Developing an Incarnational Theology of Preaching." *Homiletic* 24, no. 2 (Winter 1999): 1–12.

Holloway, Richard. *The Anglican Tradition*. Wilton, CT: Morehouse-Barlow; Toronto: Anglican Book Centre, 1984.

Hunsinger, George. "Hans Frei as Theologian: The Quest for a Generous Orthodoxy." *Modern Theology* 8, no. 2 (1992): 103–28.

Hütter, Reinhard. "The Church." In *Knowing the Triune God: The Work of the Spirit in the Practices of the Church*, edited by James J. Buckley and David S. Yeago, 23–48. Grand Rapids: Eerdmans, 2001.

———. *Suffering Divine Things: Theology as Church Practice*. Grand Rapids: Eerdmans, 2000.

Jasper, David. *A Short Introduction to Hermeneutics*. Louisville: Westminster John Knox, 2004.

Jensen, Richard. *Telling the Story: Variety and Imagination in Preaching*. Minneapolis: Augsburg, 1980.

Jenson, Robert W. "Scripture's Authority in the Church." In *The Art of Reading Scripture*, edited by Ellen F. Davis and Richard B. Hays, 27–37. Grand Rapids: Eerdmans, 2003.

———. *Visible Words: The Interpretation and Practice of Christian Sacraments*. Philadelphia: Fortress, 1978.

Jones, L. Gregory. "Embodying Scripture in the Community of Faith." In *The Art of Reading Scripture*, edited by Ellen F. Davis and Richard B. Hays, 143–47. Grand Rapids: Eerdmans, 2003.

Kay, James. *Preaching and Theology*. St. Louis: Chalice, 2007.

Keller, Catherine. *Postcolonial Theologies: Divinity and Empire*. St. Louis: Chalice, 2004.

Kelsey, David. *The Uses of Scripture in Recent Theology*. Philadelphia: Fortress, 1975.

Kolbet, Paul. *Augustine and the Cure of Souls: Revising a Classical Ideal.* Notre Dame, IN: University of Notre Dame Press, 2010.

Kysar, Robert. "New Doctrinal Preaching for a New Century." *Journal for Preachers* 20 (Easter 1997): 17–22.

Lamott, Anne. *Plan B: Further Thoughts on Faith.* New York: Riverhead Books, 2005.

Lange, Frederik. *Waiting for the Word: Dietrich Bonhoeffer on Speaking about God.* Grand Rapids: Eerdmans, 2000.

LaRue, Cleophus James. *The Heart of Black Preaching.* Louisville: Westminster John Knox, 2000.

Lash, Nicholas. *Theology on the Way to Emmaus.* London: SCM, 1986.

Legaspi, Michael. *The Death of Scripture and the Rise of Biblical Studies.* Oxford: Oxford University Press, 2010.

Lindbeck, George. "Afterword: Interreligious Relations and Christian Ecumenism: Revisiting Chapter 3 of *The Nature of Doctrine.*" In *The Nature of Doctrine: Religion and Theology in a Postliberal Age*, 125–40. 25th anniversary ed. Louisville: Westminster John Knox, 2009.

———. "The Church as Israel: Ecclesiology and Ecumenism." In *Jews and Christians: People of God*, edited by Carl E. Braaten and Robert W. Jenson, 78–94. Grand Rapids: Eerdmans, 2003.

———. *The Church in a Postliberal Age.* Edited by James J. Buckley. Grand Rapids: Eerdmans, 2003.

———. *The Nature of Doctrine: Religion and Theology in a Postliberal Age.* 25th anniversary ed. Louisville: Westminster John Knox, 2009.

Lints, Richard. *The Fabric of Theology: A Prolegomenon to Evangelical Theology.* Grand Rapids: Eerdmans, 1993.

Lischer, Richard. *The End of Words: The Language of Reconciliation in a Culture of Violence.* Grand Rapids: Eerdmans, 2008.

———. "The Limits of Story." *Interpretation* 38, no. 1 (1984): 26–38.

———. *The Preacher King: Martin Luther King, Jr. and the Word That Moved America.* Paperback ed. New York: Oxford University Press, 1997.

———. *A Theology of Preaching: The Dynamics of the Gospel.* Rev. ed. Eugene, OR: Wipf and Stock, 2001.

———. *Theories of Preaching: Selected Readings in the Homiletical Tradition.* Durham, NC: Labyrinth, 1987.

Long, Thomas G. *Preaching and the Literary Forms of the Bible.* Philadelphia: Fortress, 1989.

———. *Preaching from Memory to Hope.* Louisville: Westminster John Knox, 2009.

———. *The Witness of Preaching.* 3rd ed. Louisville: Westminster John Knox, 2016.

Long, Thomas G., and Leonora Tubbs Tisdale. *Teaching Preaching as a Christian Practice: A New Approach to Homiletical Pedagogy.* Louisville: Westminster John Knox, 2008.

Lose, David. *Confessing Jesus Christ: Preaching in a Postmodern World.* Grand Rapids: Eerdmans, 2003.

———. "Narrative and Proclamation." *Homiletic* 23, no. 1 (Summer 1998): 1–14.

Lowry, Eugene. *The Homiletical Plot: The Sermon as Narrative Art Form.* Louisville: Westminster John Knox, 1980.

Luther, Martin. *Luther's Works.* American ed. 55 vols. Edited by Jaroslav Pelikan and Helmut T. Lehmann. St. Louis: Concordia, 1955–86.

Marshall, Bruce D. "Introduction: The Nature of Doctrine after 25 Years." In *The Nature of Doctrine: Religion and Theology in a Postliberal Age*, by George A. Lindbeck, vii–xxvii. Louisville: Westminster John Knox, 2009.

———. *Theology and Dialogue: Essays in Conversation with George Lindbeck.* Notre Dame, IN: University of Notre Dame Press, 1990.

Matthews, Alice. *Preaching That Speaks to Women.* Grand Rapids: Baker Academic, 2003.

McClain, William B. *Come Sunday: The Liturgy of Zion.* Nashville: Abingdon, 1990.

McClure, John. *The Roundtable Pulpit: Where Leadership and Preaching Meet.* Nashville: Abingdon, 1995.

Mitchell, Henry H. *Black Preaching: The Recovery of a Powerful Art.* Nashville: Abingdon, 1991.

Murphy, Francesca Aran. *God Is Not a Story: Realism Revisited.* Oxford: Oxford University Press, 2007.

Norris, Kathleen. *The Quotidian Mysteries: Laundry, Liturgy and "Women's Work."* Mahwah, NJ: Paulist Press, 1998.

O'Connell, Gerard. "Francis the Preacher." *America Magazine*, December 5–12, 2016, 24.

O'Day, Gail, and Thomas G. Long, eds. *Listening to the Word: Studies in Honor of Fred B. Craddock.* Nashville: Abingdon, 1993.

Ormond, J. Will. *Preaching Eyes for Listening Ears: Sermons and Commentary for Preachers and Students of Preaching.* Lima, OH: CSS, 1999.

Owens, Roger L. "Preaching as Participation: Dietrich Bonhoeffer's Christology of Preaching." *Currents in Theology and Mission* 36, no. 1 (February 2009): 47–54.

Paddison, Angus. *Scripture: A Very Theological Proposal.* New York: T&T Clark, 2009.

Pasquarello, Michael. *Christian Preaching: A Trinitarian Theology of Proclamation.* Grand Rapids: Baker Academic, 2006.

———. *Sacred Rhetoric: Preaching as a Theological and Pastoral Practice of the Church.* Grand Rapids: Eerdmans, 2005.

Patte, Daniel. *Preaching Paul.* Philadelphia: Fortress, 1984.

Porter, Stanley E., and Beth M. Stovell, eds. *Biblical Hermeneutics: Five Views.* Downers Grove, IL: IVP Academic, 2012.

Price, Reynolds. *The Three Gospels.* New York: Scribner, 1996.

———. *A Whole New Life.* New York: Scribner, 1995.

Radner, Ephraim. "The Absence of the Comforter: Scripture and the Divided Church." In *Theological Exegesis: Essays in Honor of Brevard S. Childs*, edited by Christopher Seitz and Kathryn Greene-McCreight, 355–94. Grand Rapids: Eerdmans, 1999.

———. *Hope among the Fragments: The Broken Church and Its Engagement of Scripture.* Grand Rapids: Brazos, 2004.

———. *Leviticus.* Brazos Theological Commentary on the Bible. Grand Rapids: Brazos, 2008.

———. *Time and the Word: Figural Reading of the Christian Scriptures*. Grand Rapids: Eerdmans, 2016.

Reno, Russell. *In the Ruins of the Church: Sustaining Faith in an Age of Diminished Christianity*. Grand Rapids: Brazos, 2002.

Resner, André, Jr. *Preacher and Cross: Person and Message in Theology and Rhetoric*. Grand Rapids: Eerdmans, 1999.

Rice, Charles. *Interpretation and Imagination: The Preacher and Contemporary Literature*. Philadelphia: Fortress, 1970.

———. "The Preacher as Storyteller." *Union Seminary Quarterly Review* 31 (Spring 1976): 182–97.

Ricoeur, Paul. "The Hermeneutics of Testimony." In *Essays on Biblical Interpretation*, edited by Lewis Mudge, 119–54. Philadelphia: Fortress, 1980.

Root, Michael, and James J. Buckley, eds. *Sharper Than a Two-Edged Sword: Preaching, Teaching, and Living the Bible*. Grand Rapids: Eerdmans, 2008.

Rose, Lucy A. "Conversational Preaching: A Proposal." *Journal for Preachers* 19, no. 1 (Advent 1995): 26–30.

———. "Narrative Preaching and Biblical Criticism." *Homiletic* 17, no. 1 (Summer 1992): 1–5.

———. *Sharing the Word: Preaching in the Roundtable Church*. Louisville: Westminster John Knox, 1997.

———. *Songs in the Night*. Decatur, GA: CTS, 1998.

Saunders, Stanley P., and Charles Campbell. "Anything but Ordinary: Worship and Preaching in Ordinary Time." *Journal for Preachers* 18, no. 4 (Pentecost 1995): 25–31.

Secor, Philip. *Richard Hooker on Anglican Faith and Worship: Of the Laws of Ecclesiastical Polity, Book V*. Modern ed. London: SPCK, 2003.

Seitz, Christopher. "New Works in the Theological Interpretation of Scripture." *The Living Church*, February 27, 2011, 8–11.

Seitz, Christopher, and Kathryn Greene-McCreight, eds. *Theological Exegesis: Essays in Honor of Brevard S. Childs*. Grand Rapids: Eerdmans, 1999.

Seymour, D. Bruce. *Creating Stories That Connect: A Pastor's Guide to Storytelling*. Grand Rapids: Kregel, 2007.

Shepherd, William, Jr. *No Deed Greater Than a Word: A New Approach to Biblical Preaching*. Lima, OH: CSS, 1998.

———. "A Rickety Bridge: Biblical Preaching in Crisis." *Anglican Theological Review* 80, no. 2 (1998): 186–206.

Smith, Christine. *Preaching as Weeping, Confession, and Resistance: Radical Responses to Radical Evil*. Louisville: Westminster John Knox, 1992.

———. *Weaving the Sermon: Preaching in a Feminist Perspective*. Louisville: Westminster John Knox, 1989.

Smith, James K. A. *How (Not) to Be Secular: Reading Charles Taylor*. Grand Rapids: Eerdmans: 2014.

Steimle, Edmund, Morris Niedenthal, and Charles Rice. *Preaching the Story*. Philadelphia: Fortress, 1980.

Stott, John R. W. *Between Two Worlds: The Art of Preaching in the Twentieth Century*. Grand Rapids: Eerdmans, 1982.

Sumner, George. *Wycliffe College Handbook*. Toronto: Wycliffe College, 2010.

Tanner, Beth LaNeel. *The Book of Psalms through the Lens of Intertextuality*. Studies in Biblical Literature 26. New York: Peter Lang, 2001.

Taylor, Charles. *A Secular Age*. Cambridge, MA: Harvard University Press, 2007.

———. *Sources of the Self: The Making of Modern Identity*. Cambridge: Cambridge University Press, 1992.

Taylor, Marion, and Agnes Choi. *Handbook of Women Biblical Interpreters: A Historical and Biographical Guide*. Grand Rapids: Baker Academic, 2012.

Thompson, James A. W. "Interpreting Texts for Preaching: A New Approach to Homiletical Pedagogy." In *Teaching Preaching as a Christian Practice*, edited by Thomas G. Long and Leonora Tubbs Tisdale, 61–74. Louisville: Westminster John Knox, 2008.

Tisdale, Leonora Tubbs. *Preaching as Local Theology and Folk Art*. Minneapolis: Fortress, 1997.

Torrance, James. *Worship, Community and the Triune God of Grace*. Downers Grove, IL: InterVarsity, 1996.

Turner, Philip. *Christian Ethics and the Church: Ecclesial Foundations for Moral Thought and Practice*. Grand Rapids: Baker Academic, 2015.

———. "The Exemplary Power of Lives Well Lived: Truth and Reconciliation." In *Christian Ethics and the Church: Ecclesial Foundations for Moral Thought and Practice*, 205–11. Grand Rapids: Baker Academic, 2015.

Vanhoozer, Kevin J., ed. *Dictionary for Theological Interpretation of the Bible*. Grand Rapids: Baker Academic, 2005.

Van Seters, Art. "Dilemmas in Preaching Doctrine: Theology's Public Voice." *Journal for Preachers* 20, no. 3 (Easter 1997): 23–29.

Volf, Miroslav. *Captive to the Word of God: Engaging the Scriptures for Contemporary Theological Reflection*. Grand Rapids: Eerdmans, 2010.

Volf, Miroslav, and Dorothy C. Bass, eds. *Practicing Theology: Beliefs and Practices in Christian Life*. Grand Rapids: Eerdmans, 2001.

Wainwright, Geoffrey. "Preaching as Worship." *Greek Orthodox Theological Review* 28, no. 4 (Winter 1983): 325–36.

Watson, Francis. *Text and Truth: Redefining Biblical Theology*. Grand Rapids: Eerdmans, 1997.

———. *Text, Church, and World: Biblical Interpretation in Theological Perspective*. Grand Rapids: Eerdmans, 1994.

Webster, John. *Domain of the Word: Scripture and Theological Reason*. New York: T&T Clark, 2012.

Williams, Charles. *Descent of the Dove: A Short History of the Holy Spirit in the Church*. Eugene, OR: Wipf and Stock, 2016.

Willimon, William. *Conversations with Barth on Preaching*. Nashville: Abingdon, 2006.

———. "Postmodern Preaching: Learning to Love the Thickness of the Text." *Journal for Preachers* 19, no. 3 (Easter 1996): 32–37.

Wilson, Paul Scott. "Biblical Studies and Preaching: A Growing Divide." In *Preaching as a Theological Task: Word, Gospel, Scripture; In Honor of David Buttrick*, edited by Thomas G. Long and Edward Farley, 137–49. Louisville: Westminster John Knox, 1996.

———. *Broken Words: Reflections on the Craft of Preaching.* Nashville: Abingdon, 2004.

———. *A Concise History of Preaching.* Nashville: Abingdon, 1992.

———. *The Four Pages of the Sermon: A Guide to Biblical Preaching.* Nashville: Abingdon, 1999.

———. *Preaching and Homiletical Theory.* St. Louis: Chalice, 2004.

———. "Preaching and the Sacrament of Holy Communion." In *Preaching in the Context of Worship,* edited by David M. Greenhaw and Ronald J. Allen, 43–61. St. Louis: Chalice, 2000.

———. "Preaching at the Beginning of a New Millennium: Learning from Our Predecessors." *Journal for Preachers* 20, no. 4 (Pentecost 1997): 3–8.

Wilson, Walter T. "Journeys toward Colossae: A Biblical Model for Preaching." *Journal for Preachers* 22, no. 4 (Pentecost 1999): 29–36.

Work, Telford. *Living and Active: Scripture in the Economy of Salvation.* Grand Rapids: Eerdmans, 2001.

Wright, John. *Telling God's Story: Narrative Preaching for Christian Formation.* Downers Grove, IL: IVP Academic, 2007.

Yeago, David S. "The Bible: The Spirit, the Church and the Scriptures; Biblical Inspiration and Interpretation Revisited." In *Knowing the Triune God: The Work of the Spirit in the Practices of the Church,* edited by James J. Buckley and David S. Yeago, 49–93. Grand Rapids: Eerdmans, 2001.

Yoder, John Howard. *The Priestly Kingdom: Social Ethics as Gospel.* Notre Dame, IN: University of Notre Dame Press, 1985.

York, Hershael W., and Scott A. Blue. "Is Application Necessary in Expository Preaching?" *Southern Baptist Journal of Theology* 7 (Summer 1999): 70–84.

Index